Please note this book probably reads like 2 ½ separate
final section on year 3. The reason for this is because i
but I wanted to stitch all 3 together into one book so pe
rather than buying separate books.

Each time I wrote I think I got better, I definitely change
you read it but it's also the way I wanted the book to be ... fancy, just
entertaining which for me is what a book should be.

I hope you appreciate the reasons for me doing this and why the book feels like this.

I train because I want to defeat my self. Defeat the me who couldn't do it yesterday so I can be better today.

## Book index

Introduction

I don't really know why I'm writing this book, I didn't enjoy writing at school but I seem to spend so much time at the moment updating my status, tweeting, blogging, speaking, instagramming, and who knows how many other methods of communicating, writing a short book was perhaps the only thing left to do – perhaps an amalgamation of all those other methods, hopefully producing something which at least one person will read and maybe even, enjoy!

It will be a short book, I have a very limited attention span so will reflect this in my writing, there may be some spelling/grammar mistakes, and it may also be a little random in places, a little like me, but I'm not pretending to be a professional writer, it's just the "vanilla" version of me – not skin wrapped around it (I hear this phrase all the time with Android, not sure if it translates so well to that sentence).

I love this quote, I chose to challenge myself as I don't want to settle with being ordinary, I want to be extra-ordinary.

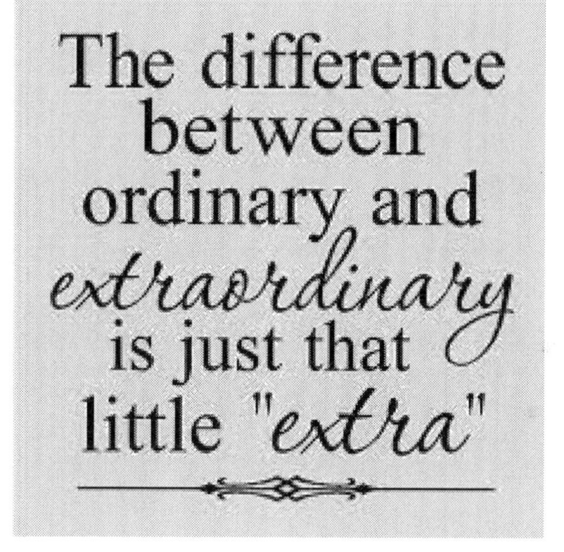

Acknowledgements

Before you move onto the first chapter, the obligatory thankyou's follow, I know these are often at the end of the book but I don't think we say thank you enough so I'm doing it first:

My mum (Mary) – thanks for bringing me into this world, thanks for doing your best bringing me up on your own, thanks for sticking with me when I've done the odd naughty thing (or two). I can never thank you enough, in fact I don't think I ever thank you – I hope I've done you proud as I've matured

My wife (Sally) – thanks for taking over from my mum, looking after me from the age of 23 and giving my poor mother a rest. You took on a real pain in the a!se guy, showed patience and kindness which I thought only my mother (maybe Mother Theresa, Ghandi , Mandela and a few other famous figures) could ever have. You've helped me through some hard times, shared with me some great times, baked loads of amazing cakes, and given me a reason to work smart, play hard, and enjoy life.

The people who have passed through my life – thanks for giving me a great life so far, both the good and bad people. I've learnt so much, what to do, what not to do, how to behave, how to treat others. At 42 years old and coming to the end of the best year of my life I want to thank you for all this life experience, without it I wouldn't appreciate all that I have

A special thanks to the people I've worked with, I've had lots of jobs and learnt lots of things through good and bad experiences. I am only as good as the people I work with or the teams I run, so thanks.

Finally, thanks to the runners I've met either face to face on races or those on social networking. Not since my bodybuilding days have I had such a good social circle, but when I left bodybuilding I took a clean break and left most of those friends, I would have been too tempted to go back otherwise. Runners are different to bodybuilders; both involve being mentally strong but also differed. Bodybuilding for me was based on aggression lifting weights, getting big and strong, running (especially trails and longer distances) is about feeling free, relaxed and happy (you can eat cake!). You are accepted for who you are, there are so many races available that it's easy to access, all you need is a T-shirt, shorts and trainers, no excuses not to try it.

Life background

In summary, born in the UK on 21 October 1972, I have a Maltese mother and a Scottish father. This combination of parents, both pretty fiery tempers, set me up well for the future – I had no choice but to be quite unpredictable, one moment I'm calm, the next moment I explode with anger, as I get older and wiser I realise the need to focus this energy on good things, it's helped me a lot in recent years in my quest to become a better person. My parents split when I was 5, my mother took on me and my brother (3 years younger than me).

I went to a local council school, I was pretty smart and one of those annoying kids who didn't need to concentrate but still did well. Unfortunately the boredom of lessons meant I looked for something more exciting, getting in all kinds of trouble as many kids do.

My mother, struggling with bringing us up on her own whilst working hard to provide for us, put me forward to what was known as the 11 Plus exam – basically an exam which results in one lucky person getting a Government assisted place to local private school. I didn't want to do this but the competitive side of me still wanted to do well in the exam, maybe showing off, and the result was – oh no, a place in a private, all boys school. I was the poor kid, hand down school uniform, unable to go on school trips, but made some good chums (a posh friend). I passed all my exams (GCSE's in the UK), signed up for A-levels but got quickly bored of those, deciding to quit after one term and go to work.

(Here I am with my mum and brother, plus me with strawberry blonde hair and Maltese pot-belly)

## Work background

I'd always worked since I was young, washing dishes for £1 an hour, retail work, cleaning, etc. When I left school I was a computer geek who loved maths, so I spent time doing book-keeping, then using my Lotus 123 skills, moved the books onto spread sheets, and eventually to Sage accounting software. This was great, I had saved myself loads of time, unfortunately so much time that I was made redundant – well not quite, I hung in there and moved to the factory floor, and I turned myself into an engineer!

I spent the next 15 years drifting aimlessly from job to job, industry to industry, with no clear career path in mind. I managed a betting shop, I worked with actuaries in life assurance, I did retail, banking, security work, even the worst job in the UK – a traffic warden!

In summary, I worked for two reasons

1. To earn some money, never well paid but I was more than happy to do as many hours as it would take to bring in good money at the end of the week. I believe in owning what I needed, but not what I want – by this I mean I try to stick to the things I need to live on, not the luxuries which people lust after. I believe this is where the tipping point towards greed comes about, I went down that route in the past and become quite a nasty person, I do my best not to go down that path again
2. To enjoy life, if I enjoy work then work doesn't feel like effort, and if something is effortless (or a least partly effortless), this is the state of mind for your best work. I remember resigning from a job as a manager in a bank, people asked me why I was doing this as it was very sudden, I answered by telling them I didn't enjoy the job any more – I was leaving to work nights in a supermarket instead. Some people couldn't understand this; I was leaving a good employee, a good job title, a decent salary, to work nights in a supermarket for much less money! Money does not bring happiness, it brings greed, stress, and a more complex life, things I can do without

As I mentioned before, I met Sally aged 23, previously I did the same with relationships as I did with jobs, drifted from one to the other (possibly had more jobs than girlfriends though). She put up with me working on the doors of nightclubs for almost 10 years, pretty much every weekend, Christmas and New Year. We got married when I was 31, I gave up the nightclubs and decided to get a proper job – taking a pay cut to join an insurance company.

I'm proud to say I worked my backside off, moving quickly from job to job within the same company, being given a chance by several people along the way and supported by some great people, and eventually found myself a niche role in the company – Head of Continuous Improvement for Europe, Middle East and Africa. I love my job; I've visited so many countries and met loads of fabulous people. I have a great boss who has taught me a lot, am treated so well by her and the company, I try to repay this by doing the best I can almost every day (everyone has an off day). Not bad for someone with a limited academic background and no insurance knowledge, hope I did you proud mum ☺

Sport background

I love sports; at school I did football, rugby and athletics. I was pretty strong, pretty short, quite heavy, and eventually found a love for the gym. I had a stupid goal when I was young, match my age with my bodyweight – 15 years old, 15 stone, and so on. I got stronger and stronger, joining a local powerlifting gym, learning correct form, and growing like a weed – this translated into extra aggression, not good when working as a nightclub doorman (sorry to all those customers I had altercations with; it was always your fault though). I would bench press over 210kg, squat and deadlift over 300kg, but I weighed over 20 stone (280lb/125kg).

Aged 30 I had a slight wobble while walking down the street, not sure if it was my heart warning me and just general bad fitness, but I decided to do something about it. I left the powerlifting gym, went to one with cardio machines (even showers/changing room!), and started to peel off the weight. Within 6 months I'd dropped close to 5 stone (90lb/40kg), and someone joked to me that I should enter a bodybuilding show. I took that as a challenge; stripped off a bit more weight, shaved myself head to toe, slapped on some fake tan, oil and glitter, and turned up at one of the UK's largest regional shows. I'm not an exhibitionist, I cover myself up on a beach, I don't dance, and the nerves were getting to me backstage as I sat there in a Guinness T-Shirt and scruffy tracksuit bottoms, watching these guys in fantastic shape warm up – even a personal trainer/ex-marine who looked after one of the Spice Girls was in the same class as me. Anyway I got up on stage, the lights blinded me so much I couldn't see the 1000+ people in the audience, and I posed my ar#e off – what more could I do, I had no choice, I wasn't going to stand there looking scared. Amazingly I won that show, 6 months later I was at the British Finals at placed 3rd in my class, and I found fame. Sponsorship, magazine, newspaper and TV followed, I was winning or placing in shows without having to work that hard for it, I was a natural, but as expectations grew I drifted further away from the reason I joined this sport in the first place. I loved lifting weights with my mates, I loved eating food, I enjoyed every minute of that, but the pressure of performing on stage, staying in shape for sponsors, and being skint (bodybuilders don't get paid, the people who run shows and sell supplements make the cash), made me one miserable person with a really, really, bad temper.

I can't believe I lasted 3 years as a bodybuilder without losing Sally; I was a self-obsessed, moody, unpredictable, bad husband. She has the patience of a saint, the nicest, kindest person I know.

I decided to quit when I contracted blood poisoning, got septicaemia, and was in danger of either losing my entire right arm, or worse still, death (no joke). I had also just got married, moved to my new career focussed job, and was basically upsetting everyone at work. I made the decision to quit bodybuilding while I was ahead – I qualified for the British finals, went up there with the sole intention of enjoying the experience one last time. I got a load of free supplements off my sponsors (never told them I was quitting), got in what I thought was the best shape of my life (mentally I was really happy, body wise I looked good), and did my last show with a tear in my eye – all my previous shows I'd done my posing to angry, rock music, for this last show I used Hero by Henrique Englesius (one of Sally's favourite songs).

Everyone I had to do with bodybuilding was left at that show, all the supplements were given away, magazines went in the bin, and I wanted a clean break. For 2 years I hardly stepped into a gym, rarely ate meat (a nice break after eating a kilo of meat a day for so long), and concentrated on my new career.

When I did eventually start back in a gym, I trained with Sally. By doing this I removed any temptation to train heavy (she's tiny). As my career took off, I travelled more and more, finding it harder to get to a gym, so I took up running – trainers, T-shirt and shorts packed in my suitcase, find a road to run on, there's no excuse. I found a new sport to enjoy, it was free, easy, healthy, and I could do it in any country I was working in (I've worked in pretty much every country in Europe in the last 4 years, from Portugal all the way across to Russia).

This is how I've transformed from overweight powerlifter, to bodybuilder, to bodybuilder-type runner – I'm quite proud of this, plus the last picture of me onstage (felt really sad this day, end of an era, time to grow up)

Garmin day 40th birthday, Toronto

My wife and I always go on holiday for our birthdays; we have no kids so we just do as we please. For my 40th we went to Toronto, a fabulous place, and we went in the autumn during the fall – Sally loves this time of year, when the leaves change colour and the air feels cleaner. I don't have much stress in my life, but one of the biggest causes of stress is when I get asked "what do you want for your birthday/Xmas?" I honestly need nothing, I am a firm believer in differentiating between want you need and what you want. I need nothing, there are things I want but this is out of greed – when I think back to when I worked hard and earned less, there were things I wanted out of greed but couldn't afford, I could live without them and had a great life, so even though I have more disposable income I still think twice before buying such luxuries.

Anyway, Sally had noticed I was running more, she knows how I love maths and measuring things (part of my day job), so bought me a Garmin GPS watch. Ungrateful I told her to return it, I could run fine without a watch, but I saw how disappointed she was (as always, she had put a lot of thought in this, probably stresses out more than me over this), so I eventually accepted the watch and started running with it.

Why am I running?

Measuring stats such as distance, heartbeat, elevation, and even learning the difference between speed and pace, took hold of me – I wasn't returning the watch. I would pound the streets, setting myself a goal in 2013 to run at least 26 miles every week for the year. After 297 runs I hit this goal, and then thought to myself "what have I achieved through this?" Probably over-analysing things, but I refuse to do things unless I have a reason/purpose.

Was the purpose to lose weight? Well if it was I'd failed

Was it to win races? I'd not entered any races

Was it to replace the gym? I still went to the gym

Was it to make friends? I run on my own, so no

I got frustrated with this, when I run I think a lot, and on cold days when I was running and kept asking myself "why?"

I had got into reading about psychology, Buddhism, doing yoga, and other spiritual stuff. This complicated the question even further, was I trying to run away from something, get away from the demons of my past or to forget something ? I looked deep into myself, realising that there was a small gap that potentially I was trying to fill – to find myself a more fulfilled life, become a happier, nicer, more approachable person, and to in turn motivate others to try doing something that challenges them. I settled on this as the reason for running – not sure if it was the only reason, but it was enough for now.

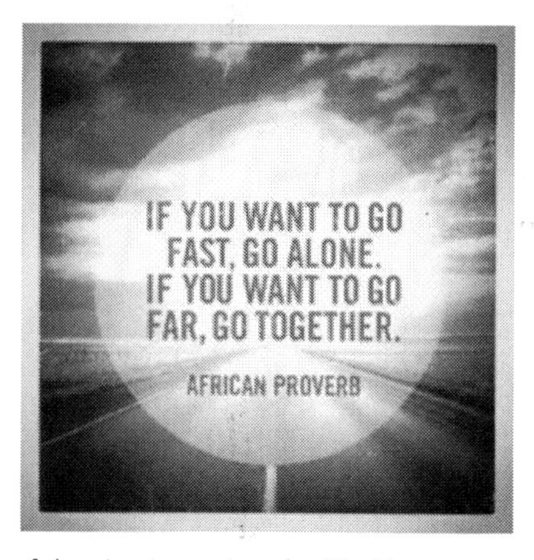


Fast forward to February 2014 – sat at work opposite one of the nicest guys I work with. He was training for triathlons and mentioned he was doing the Portsmouth Coastal half marathon soon. I asked him what time he was aiming at; sub 2 hours was his answer. Reverting to the nasty side of me, I found myself laughing in my head at this – sub 2 hours! I had run 13 miles sub 1 hr. 45 mins for fun. I read a lot about acknowledging your sub-conscious self, and when I got home and was running I thought back to this sniggering, realising what a total d!ck I was. When I was bodybuilding I despised those people who sat in the audience, with the tight T-shirts on, criticising those on stage – yes you may have bigger muscles than him but you're sat in the audience, you've never competed, so that makes your competition history even worse than the person who came last on stage. I had worked hard to become a better person but old habits are hard to break, I was no better than these people, turning to my conscious self I had to do something to correct this, so I entered the Portsmouth Coastal half.

Portsmouth Coastal Half
Sunday February $23^{rd}$ 2014

So after having run 13.1 miles many times in the past, this was my first real race. It was in aid of the RNLI, being a coastal town a very suitable charity. I saw my friends mentioned above at the start line but avoided him; I didn't want him to know I was doing this in case I screwed up. I stupidly pushed myself right to the front of the runners, at the start line waiting for the gun to go off, and when it did, wow!

I found speed I'd never reached in training, keeping with the leading pack and in my heading even daring to think I could get a top 3 place. 1km went, 2km, 3km, and then wow again! I ran out of gas, couldn't feel my legs, and started getting over-taken by other runners. The race went from seafront promenade to what was known as "The Muddy Beach" which really was muddy, peoples shoes were coming off. We then ran into a headwind along pavement, onto grass, onto the beach, and then back along the seafront. All the time I was being overtaken, but I was still moving. I eventually got overtaken by enough people to find my natural level, I started keeping up with people, less overtook me, and I even overtook some myself. This motivated me; I got a second wind, and actually crossed the line finishing not too bad.

I felt so chuffed at the end; I'd finished in 1h 38m, placed $68^{th}$ out of 761 runners (top 10%). I didn't enjoy the race but enjoyed the feeling at the end, the endorphins were working overtime, and I couldn't wait until the next race (not yet entered). This was a really well run race, a good medal, decent goodie bag, I can see why it's so popular. Lessons learnt from this race, a) I can complete a race, b) I need to slow down at the start, c) I need to fuel up a little better.

Portsmouth Coastal
HALF MARATHON
Eastern Road
Gun Wharf
Goldsmith Avenue
Portsmouth
RNLI Station
Muddy Beach
Round Tower
Royal Marines Museum
Albert Road
Clarence Pier
Start & Finish Pyramids Centre
Eastern Parade
Southsea Castle
South Parade Pier
Key
Car Park
Water Fuel Station
Toilets
Miles Out

John Austin Half Sunday March 9th 2014

So when I got home from the Portsmouth Coastal, still buzzing, I immediately began to look for a new race – quantity vs. quality, I was choosing quantity. The one thing I didn't really like about the Portsmouth race was that it was mostly on pavement, not good for my joints, not really stimulating my senses, so I decided to hunt down a trail race. I found the John Austin half in the New Forest, Dorset, which was in aid of the John Austin Hospice, it was only a few weeks after my first race but what the hell, who needs rest, I felt not too bad after the last one to I'm sure I'll be fine.

We had a bit further to travel this time, about an hour away, so Sally and I set off early, the race HQ was at Brockenhurst college, the sports hall was full of lots of "mature" people who greeted us real friendly, I registered on the day with two of them and then went to prepare myself.

My preparation for this race was the same as the first, but on the day I felt a little tired so I took some pre-workout stimulant drink, ibuprofen, aspirin, and god knows what else. We had a mile walk to the start like; it was all trail and muddy in places. I didn't learn my lesson from the first race; yet again I pushed myself to the front. The gun went off, I roared off at a pace, but this time the trail and slight incline made me suffèr much earlier – I don't think I even lasted a km before struggling.

There was no way I was giving up so I dug in, the potion I took before the race took hold, and to be honest most of the race I don't remember, I was in a dream (or is that "in the zone"), and all I remember is needing the toilet for most of the race. I got to about 11 miles and couldn't hold on any longer, luckily being a trail race there's plenty of bushes to hide in so I took advantage of this and then finished the race.

The biggest memory of this race is me crossing the finish line, in quite a bit of pain (the ibuprofen had worn off), and telling Sally I couldn't remember much of those 13.1 miles and I had been stupid to even enter it – too soon after the last one. I also remember a really tiny, I think Spanish, lady who glided through the course so fast. The reason I remembered her is that I had been using an excuse that I was short and my stride length was not wide, hence me not being so fast, but having seen her my excuse was blown out of the water – time to look for a new one.

I finished in a time of 1 hr. 39m, 92nd out of 531 (well inside my top 20% goal) not so bad I guess. The race was yet again really well run, a friendly atmosphere, a good turnout, a nice area of the country to run. Lessons learnt, plan my racing better in future!

Three Forts Half Sunday 4th May 2014

So this was my 3rd half marathon race of the year, it is known as one of the toughest in the country (I know, many claim this). Again it was trail, this time across 3 hills, and was held in Worthing, Dorset, which is maybe an hour drive away, but east of our house (previous race was west).

In preparation for this race Sally and I actually drove to the venue a week before so I knew where the race HQ was. Ashamed to say it's less than an hour drive away from my home but I don't tend to travel so much around the UK so to remove any stress on race day I thought it prudent to do this.

The location was really easy to find, we decided to walk some of it to see what the terrain was like, wasn't sure if this was a good idea since I knew the course was labelled one of the toughest around (there are so many who tag themselves with similar so it tends to lose impact), if the course looked too tough would I get more nervous than I was already? The course started up a steep, narrow track, very uneven underfoot, but then at the top you get to the point that I love in races – the most fantastic views of the South Downs National Park, as well as down to the Solent channel. I love walking trails, now I love running trails; the toughness of racing on them is easily overcome by the locations. Anyway, we ended up walking a couple of hours, totally lost track of the course but had a great time and then we participated in my second favourite hobby, eating a picnic on the South Downs.

A week later we headed off to the race HQ early; I had taken on board the learning from our visit last week and bought my first pair of trail shoes. I felt really motivated for this race, well fuelled up, organisation at the start was great, I got talking to some fellow athletes, and I had my support crew (Sally, my wife) by my side carrying my race bag which as usual was packed with far too much, nothing too wrong with over preparing is there ?

The race set off shortly after the marathon race; well in fact it's a mile further than a marathon so technically a (short) ultra. I took on board learning's from the previous 2 races, setting myself back from the people at the front of the start line, aiming for top 20% so started roughly that far back from the front. This caused some problems at the start as it was straight up a hill for a couple of km, very uneven, deep ruts in the middle, single file only. I had been practicing hills leading up to this and felt really good as we started to climb, the problem was having started a little back in the pack I found myself in a long queue, behind some people who, like me in the last two races, were maybe a little too enthusiastic and struggled right at the start. As a result of this the first 3km took me 16 ½ minutes, almost 140m climb, not a great start.

Once at the top of the hill the route opened up, along the top of the hill and then back down towards first welcome checkpoint, still uneven ground but I had my new trail shoes on so felt more stable than I would have otherwise. Whilst the shoes were helping with grip, they also felt uncomfortable, I put this down to the fact this was the first time I'd worn them, stupid thing to do but I only bought them the day before so had no choice.

Anyway, the rest of the race went well, my feet hurt but I figured this was the new shoes, the uneven ground, and the hills (some of which I still had to walk up, a good strategy as I can walk pretty quick plus on the downhill I'd always overtake anyone who had passed me going up). The route was circular, so the last few km were back down the hill I'd been caught up on at the start. I was running behind another guy, we were running pretty fast downhill and pushing each other hard, however with the ground being so uneven, and my own personal values telling me it was un-sportsmanlike to tailgate someone then overtake at the last moment, I eased off in case I damaged myself (my feet were killing me by this stage), finishing in 1h 47m, average of just over 5 min/km, 62$^{nd}$ out of 377 (inside my top 20% goal again).

Sally was there waiting when I finished, I immediately had to kick off my shoes to allow my feet to relax, what I saw was quite alarming. I peeled off my socks and two toenails peeled back, on top of that I had 3 huge blood blister on my heals and top of my toe. I knew the shoes were hurting, I didn't realise just how much until then. Initially I put this down to my socks which had twisted and not fitting so well, but then I realised something really basic – the shoes I had bought were what I thought were half a size larger than my standard size, 8.5, however it was only now that I noticed the shoe size was American, so I'd in fact worn shoes half a size too small, no wonder my feet were in a mess. This didn't distract from what was a great race, well run, great weather, nice views, cake at the end.

Learning points from this race were a) beware of narrow hills, b) beware of American shoe sizes, c) keep practicing hills.

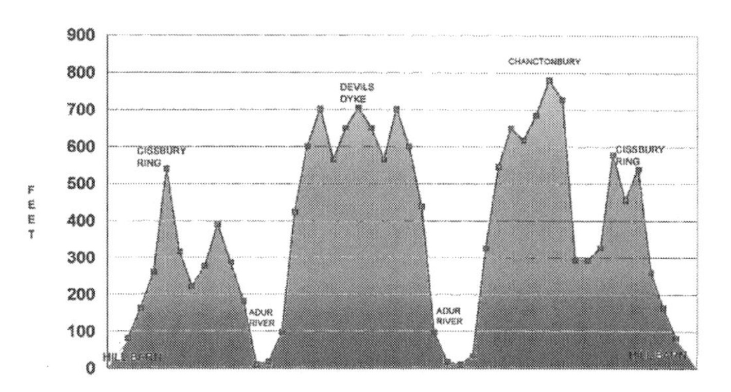
Three Forts Ascent Profile
900
800
700
600
500
400
300
200
100
0
FEET
CISSBURY RING
DEVILS DYKE
CHANCTONBURY
CISSBURY RING
ADUR RIVER
ADUR RIVER

Stansted Slog Half Sunday 20th July 2014

So after a whole month of now running (we went to Dominican Republic on holiday, all inclusive so far too much food and alcohol), I returned to racing in July. Another trail, hills, and half marathon distance. Stansted House is just around the corner from where I live so no pre-race recce required, the only thing I was unsure of was how I'd cope with 13.1 miles after a holiday. In preparation I tried 13 miles a week after returning from holiday, I had to run/walk it, and then I tried again a week later, again run/walk but slightly better, so in my head I knew I'd complete the race, the run/walk wouldn't be a problem since I'd use this strategy on the hills again.

This race is organised by our local Portsmouth Joggers Club, I don't belong to this club (or any other club), however through racing and social media I'd got to know quite a few members. I recognised some friendly faces at the start so had a good chat with them beforehand whilst also swigging back my latest nutritional experiment – beetroot juice, which I had heard was good for running due to its nitrates, I took on board half a litre of the stuff. The last few races I'd stuck to quite a basic pre-race nutrition plan, carb deplete for 2 to 4 days, do some short sharp runs to burn off glycogen, then carb up for 24 to 72 hours and run less. This seemed to work but I love experimenting, hence the beetroot.

I don't remember too much of this race, it was pretty tough, my pace over 75% of the course was good at sub 5 min/km, however I really did struggle over the hills, several km's were 6:30 or worse. I put this down to the holiday, getting complacent with the walking of hills, some pretty bad cramps (warm day), and also a bad stomach.

Thankfully I managed to complete the race in 1 hr. 51 min, which was within the time limit of 2 hrs. which I set myself as a personal goal for half marathons, 36th out of 159 runners (first time I'd failed top 20%).

When I crossed the line my stomach was really playing up – I said to Sally it felt like a washing machine with water moving back or forth inside it. Sorry for the crude detail however it has to be told as it's also quite funny, straight off to the toilets I went, up to the urinal which was like a cattle trough with a load of other runners stood next to me, and I released what I thought was a trail of bloody urine. I started to panic, blood in urine was always on the radio and TV, its bad and something to worry about and I hate going to the doctors. I felt conscious that the other runners were now also seeing a river of red urine passing before them so I left to toilets quickly to see Sally. When I explained what had happened she laughed, my irrational thinking had failed to spot the obvious, Sally was a little calmer and told me it was beetroot! Of course, half a litre had been stuck in my gut; it had stained my insides just as it stains my hands when on the outside, what a relief. I don't think I will try that tactic again, I don't think it helped me, but I will still enjoy beetroot (usually grown from our allotment) in food – salads, smoothies and cake.

Key learning's a) either don't overindulge on holiday or enter a race shortly after an all-inclusive holiday, and b) no more beetroot !

Harting 10 mile trail Sunday August 3rd 2014

Just 2 weeks after the Stansted race I was back running a hilly trail race, this was as a personal punishment to myself, my performance over hills was not good enough, I was getting lazy at them, not even attempting some – just deciding to walk them. I figured a slightly shorter race would be ideal to push me towards getting better at hills, Harting was a pretty little village just up the road so no excuses.

We recced the course location during the week before the race, parked at the start line which was at the base of a hill (hills at the start of races seem to be a common thing), and told Sally I was going to run up the hill to see what kind of terrain it was as I wasn't sure whether to use trail or road shoes. I did 10k while Sally sat patiently in the car waiting, I didn't follow the course route very well, getting lost quite quickly at the top of the hill, however it at least proved to me that road shoes would be fine. The weather forecast was fine so wouldn't have to worry about mud or flooding (the Stansted had both). We set off back home about 6:30pm, the journey home should have taken about 20 minutes however to our dismay there had been a huge accident on the motorway, a lorry returning from a local abattoir with a load of dead sheep had turned over, the load had been spread across the motorway – gross! As a result the motorway was closed off, in rush hour, and therefore every driver heading north and south had turned off into the country roads, often single track only, and the entire area became gridlocked. I think it took us 3 hours or more to get home ☹

The day of the race we had no similar traffic problems; I started off about 20% back from the front runners again, and started climbing the hill. To my amazement I found the first mile, with 77m of ascent, really easy, completing it in less than 8 minutes. I then sped up, ducking under 4:30 min/km pace, then at mile 6 we faced what felt like a huge hill – 2 miles, 125 metres of ascent. My over enthusiasm earlier in the race and not having any fuel with me, meant I was pretty wiped out by this point, I tried to run/walk rather than walk the hill, averaging 5m30sec/km pace, which was pretty good compared to previous races, I was improving, but still not enough to run the entire thing.

I crossed the line just under 1 hr. 15 mins, 57th out of 206 (again, outside of top 20%, not good), average pace 4m47sec/km, so was well happy with that. Apart from telling myself to keep practicing hills, and keep entering hilly races, I learnt little else here apart from that I was enjoying running more and more – not sure why I was enjoying it, I'd lost every race, but my mental strength was becoming fantastic, never giving up, and this was transferring to my day job.

It was around this time that I started to pick up a pain in the sole of my foot, in the mornings I could hardly stand up or walk down the stairs without feeling discomfort. The pain would reduce as the day went on, never disappearing but becoming manageable, so I decided to continue without seeking medial race. I didn't relate the fact that the last 2 races I had failed to hit top 20%, putting it down to tougher courses, not an injury, but I later found out that this condition was a common runners injury known as plantar fasciitis, a stiffening of the muscles at the base of your

foot. Despite the help of Google, I didn't pay any attention to the advice to rest or support it; instead I paid more attention to the stretching element, something which I rarely did beforehand. This injury stayed with me right up to the end of the year, I used my mind (and pain killers) to overcome it, something I learnt to regret later on – my mother always said I don't listen to advice, what a hard lesson this time !

1st Park Run 5k Saturday August 13th 2014

I know some people will say technically this is not a race, however to me it is – it's running with a group of people, trying to beat times, positions, etc.

For those of you who don't know about Park Run then Google it, it's an awesome initiative which has spread worldwide. Groups of people get together on a Saturday at 9am across the world and simply run 5k. No entry fee, no online entry, you just register on the internet, get a barcode, print it off and turn up to one near you. You could be working in another country, visiting friends in another area of the country, or just fancy a day out, and turn up at one nearby. Some people do this for the social aspect, others as training for other events, some for keep fit/weight loss, and some really do treat them as races setting times I could only dream of.

Where I live we have at least 4 within a 20 minute drive. I decided to break my Park Run duck at the Southsea park run, an out and back run along the seafront. I'm pretty good at 5k on the treadmill, I don't run them too often as I prefer to plod over longer distances, and had my next race planned for the following day (Isle of Wight half marathon), so this was meant to just be a slow 5k, my final run before my race.

Me being stupid I could not resist it, surrounded by other runners I couldn't help but to compete. I started off holding back but as people overtook me my ego took over, I sped up, battling the wind on the way back, and crossing the line in 20 mins 5 seconds. I was gutted I didn't break 20 mins, I'd done this loads on the treadmill but that's not proper running.

I really enjoyed the casual atmosphere around this race, vowing to return and do some more, some of the other local ones were across hills and trails which would be great. The plan was to do these over the winter as I wasn't planning any long runs over this period – this plan was ruined in December, more to follow.

Isle of Wight Half Marathon Sunday August 17th 2014

So the day after the Park Run we headed across the Solent to the Isle of Wight. We cycled to the ferry and then to the race HQ. I entered this race; my 4th in 4 weeks (including Park Run) as the Isle of Wight is hilly so would continue to test my hill running. It wasn't a trail race which wasn't ideal, I don't like road running, but the scenery is beautiful.

Reading up on the race beforehand I'd seen the start can be a little chaotic, we gather along the seafront, the road is not closed off to traffic (not is any of the route) and then a horn goes off and you go. Keeping this in mind I pushed myself a little further towards the front of the runners, not right in front but I knew it would be quite fast so a little further than usual.

The race wasn't as hilly as I'd thought, just 235 metres of elevation vs. 265 metres at the Harting race a couple of weeks earlier. I think being a road race also helped, the terrain wasn't an issue, in fact the only thing that was an issue was nutrition – from memory I remember just a few water stations, some with cups of water (why do they put drinks in flimsy plastic cups, I spill most of the water), and others with sponges (great idea!). It was a race very popular with club runners, I felt a little out of my depth, the pace was pretty quick, but I stuck with it. Towards the end I remember catching up with another runner, slowing down and chatting away to him, proudly telling him how many races I'd run in what was my first year of racing, asking him about his own race goals, etc. I love talking, even when running, but the poor guy had enough of me after a couple of km, telling me that he was holding me back and to run off. I took the hint and left him, crossing the finishing just before the heavens opened, feeling pretty good and achieving my goal – another sub 2 hour half marathon (finish time 1 hr. 40 min), 72nd out of 333 (top 21%, getting closer to top 20% again), but more importantly I ran every inch of the race, no walking ! This was an important mental barrier for me to overcome, I can run a hilly 13.1 miles non-stop, as my next race was going to be much harder – a half marathon across the North Downs in Surrey.

We ended the day back on the mainland, going to a friend's 30th birthday party, enjoying some much welcome cake – I love cake.

Farnham Pilgrim Trail Full Marathon Sunday September 21st 2014

So I closed the report on the IOW half saying my next race was the Farnham half marathon, but the title of this says Full Marathon, have I made a mistake

Well the morning after finishing the IOW half I set off early for my recovery run, all I planned was a short 5 miles, but for some reason I continued running once I got to 5 miles – and ended up running 13 miles in 1 hr. 45m (no fuel with me). That meant I'd run marathon distance within 24 hrs., in my head I saw that as I'd run a marathon but had a big rest in the middle, mentally it was telling me I was fit enough to run a marathon (I'd actually run 26.2 miles once in 2013 during a training run). I told Sally what I'd done when she got home and told her that I felt that not only had I become lazy over hills, but also regarding challenging myself regarding distance – 13.1 miles was now nothing more than a training run. Having said that, I then looked at the Farnham race and questioned why Having said that, I then looked at the Farnham race and questioned why I was doing it, it wasn't going to challenge me, although the North Downs did look fabulous (I'd never been there). There was a full marathon option as well so I contacted the organisers, checked I could upgrade my race, they warned me it was a tough one for my first attempt but I said I'd be fine so paid the extra and that was it – my first ever marathon was entered ☺

I'd driven through Farnham but never stopped there. It was about 80km away from home, I didn't bother with a recce, and I just gave myself plenty of time to get there and turned up with Sally by my side, looking forward to a new challenge.

I loved this race, it was trail, and it was more hills than I'd done before at 566 metre elevation, it was twice as far as I'd race before. Mentally it really challenged me, there were times I wanted to stop, it was a warm day, and I sweated a lot, and experienced cramps throughout. This proved to be my biggest problem, not the distance; the first time was when I had to climb over a gate, lifted my leg up and doubled up in pain. From then on I had to try crossing further gates with a straight leg, and when climbing hills I couldn't put too much force down as my leg would feel so sore.

I remember getting to the 13 mile point, where my races usually end, and coming up against one long hill over around 4 miles, about 200 metres of ascent. Not only was this cruel, usually I was crossing the line at this point, but the course was not just trail but also consisted of a lot of sand – the whole hill was sand, with a church at the top. I did have to walk towards the top of this hill, I didn't feel bad about this as most other runners were doing the same, and my pace still averaged around 5min 30sec per km (sorry about switching between miles and km's throughout this book).

I also remember one point in the race where I was running all on my own, it was like a viaduct, and I was thinking deeply as I ran. In my head I was questioning if I'd get through the race, looking for some mental strength to keep me going, and I looked to the sky for some help (I'm not uber religious but I do believe in God). Amazingly, on a bridge ahead of me, was a cross, and not only that but as I looked at the cross the clouds moved to one side and the sun came out. Running does funny things to you sometimes, it's true about the mental side being at least, if not more, important than the physical side, especially as the distance gets longer, so I took this as a sign and found a second wind. This is the actual cross I saw

I got to mile 20 in a pretty good state; I was running with a small group of other runners, chatting away, when we hit another hill in a forest. I mentioned to the others that I was getting worse cramps and it was testing me as we climbed the hill, just as I said this I stumbled and fell to the floor, letting out a pretty pathetic yelp as I fell down hard on my outstretched hands. Once on the floor the cramp got worse, I was in real pain but still tried to look macho. The others stopped and asked if I wanted some help, I refused telling them to carry on without me, I'd be okay. I lay there trying to massage out the cramps, I think I was there for about 5 minutes, telling myself there was no way I was giving up with just 6 miles to go. My leg was cut up, I had hurt my hands falling on them, but I was still telling myself I had the choice of being 6 miles away from completing my first marathon, or giving up and then being 26.2 miles away from completing my first marathon.

Easy choice, I continued with a picture of the terminator in my head, when he's like a man on a mission chasing after the other bad guy. Amazingly I caught the others, surprising them as I started chatting to them again, they couldn't believe I was still going. Truth is I'd busted a gut trying to just get these last 6 miles out the way as quick as possible, I was knackered but not giving up, I was definitely struggling.

We headed into the final mile together, I had to slow down but crossed the line in 3 hr. 46 minutes (42nd out of 347, top 12%), beaten by mostly club runners, amazing even if I say so myself. I collapsed on the floor in a lot of pain at the end, the cramps were in my legs and also now in my stomach. I was outstretched on the floor, couldn't even think about eating any of the lovely cake on offer (it was THAT bad), and trying to be polite to fellow runners who were coming up and congratulating me.

Eventually the cramps became less painful, I had cake, and Sally drove me home. As we were heading home I told her that it felt good to complete the race but not great. I'd joined a load of other friends who had completed a marathon. The organisers were correct, it was tough, but I wanted to do something harder – I'd been joining some Ultra running Facebook pages, the romance of running further, across distances further than I'd ever imagined possible on foot, wearing really cool gear (the word buff was now in my vocabulary!), and my goal for 2015 had been set to join this group of people, but why wait until next year? Anything could happen between now and then, I was fit now, I had 3 months left in 2014, I felt in pain after the marathon but I knew if my life depended on it I could have continued further. It was at that point I decided to live to motto "Carpe Diem", I would live the day and enter an ultra in 2014.

Farnham Pilgrim Marathon 21/09/14 3h 51m

Learning point from this was simple, cramps. Learn more about how to limit them, get over them when they occur. Stretching, hydration, potassium and salts is what I learnt, I ordered salt capsules for my next race.

Stort Trail 30 mile Sunday October 26th 2014

We had been on holiday for Sally's birthday in June and planned to do the same for my birthday in October, as we do every year. This year was different, after the all-inclusive break and my set back in fitness I didn't want to go on holiday, I wanted to achieve my goal of running an ultra-marathon instead. I searched the internet and found what I thought would be a sensible introduction to ultra-running – 30 miles along a canal in Hertfordshire, in my head this meant it was further than the Farnham marathon, my flatter, so overall should be pretty easy – slightly naïve but I hope you get what I mean. The only downside was it was 5 days after my birthday so no celebrating until afterwards.

I continued using the same marathon training plan as I'd used before, the FIRST schedule which is a 3 day a week schedule, but then also for some bizarre reason decided to do 4 weeks on another 5 day a week schedule, ending up doing the FIRST schedule in the morning, and the other one in the evening. I even did a 26 mile training running leading up to the race, it wasn't part of the training schedule but I just wanted to check that completing the last marathon wasn't a fluke, that I could dig deep when running on my own – I did it !

The race was in Hertfordshire, I'd only been there once before, so made the decision to drive up a day early and we stay in a beautiful farmhouse the night before. I had no idea what nutrition to take for this race, we loaded up the car with far too much food and then I bought a load more at a local supermarket. The race was like a food crawl with running in-between, check points every 5 miles with so much food and liquid on board, I had taken food with me in my utility belt but never needed any until towards the end. I also had no idea what shoes to wear, it was labelled as trail but was flat, I decided on trail shoes – in truth I'd probably have been better off with road shoes. I also treated myself to a new Garmin watch, the 220, so that I could set pace alerts – I hoped this would help me on the longer distance.

So the race, how did it go? I loved it! It was the most social run I've ever done, running with a group for the first 17 km, using my new watch to aim at 8 min 45 second / km for this first section. Of course I totally ignored the vibrating and beeping watch at the start, running sub 7 min/km pace, but then slowing down as I lead our group and talking. Once we got past 1/3rd distance the next pacing schedule kicked in, 15 seconds/km faster than before, so I had to leave my first group and ran with another guy. Things went fine, 25 km done, at the halfway point where you turn around and head back. The guy I'd been running with was experienced; he had his camelpak on and didn't need to stop for fuel, whereas I maybe overindulged at this halfway point check point. I headed back the way I came, mentally this made things easier as I could see points that I'd passed before, every step was a step closer home. It was also good seeing runners heading in the opposite direction, not from a macho perspective thinking how far ahead I was of them, but because we'd cheer each other as we passed.

Running along canal meant navigation was easy, just keep next to the water, however there was one point at which I crossed a bridgè and then had water either side of me. Inevitably I took a wrong turn, I continued running thinking to myself a) where are all the other runners, and b) I don't remember this place? After a couple of km's it dawned on me I was lost, so I headed back to the bridge and then set off along the correct route. My pace was still okay but dropping, cramps were under control due to my learning points from previous race, but I was struggling. I ran with other athletes who towed me along, the final few miles, where I got into new virgin territory with regards to mileage, were tough and I ended up run/walking. I remember talking to myself as I walked along by myself, similar to the marathon where I kept telling myself to continue going, I was just a few miles from completing my first ultra. I was overtaken by a few runners, not too many, and then as I approached the finish I pushed myself to run up the road, a lap around the field, and across the finish line.

I ended this race in 4 hr. 34 minutes, just outside my goal of 4 hr. 30 mins, 41st out of 199 starters so top 20%) Not too bad !

Loads of lovely cake, a warm shower, and a few cups of tea, and I felt pretty fresh. Sally was due to drive home but it was a little further than she was used to so I offered to drive, we set off just over an hour after crossing the finishing line, as we drove down the road we passed some of the runners from the first group I ran with – kudos for them digging in. The organisers of this race, Challenge Running, deserve a special mention, really looked after the runners well, thank you.

Learning point from this race was that I am able to now run further than I ever thought possible, it would always be tough but in a good way, it was not only having an effect on my mental strength and my work, but also on me as a person – I felt like I was become a nicer person, more time to help people, more relaxed (relaxed when running, you wouldn't think it if you saw my face or could read my mind, it's maybe a different kind of relaxation – almost spiritual where you at one with yourself).

Gosport Half Marathon Sunday November 16th 2014

When I entered the Portsmouth Coastal at the start of the year I also entered the Gosport half at the end of the year. The plan back then was to do 2 local races, this one is known as good for pb's, but my goals had since changed – I now wanted to chase new experiences and challenges over longer distances to make not only my body but also my mind tougher, no longer were speed or personal bests important, and definitely not flat road races which were full of club runners (over 2,000 entrants!). I decided to change my training plan to short runs, running a few fast 5k's on the treadmill to get ready for The plantar fasciitis which had been bothering me for months was now much less painful which was great, but the problem with switching to a faster, shorter, running programme so quickly (sub 20min 5k's on the treadmill) was that I transferred stress onto my shins, not helped through some new minimalist style running shoes. I ignored these warning signs and carried on the training, something which will come back to haunt me later on in the year.

The week before the race, and indeed on race day, weather was absolutely terrible, giving me the ideal excuse to decide not to do this, but to have a "did not start" was not an option so I turned up deciding to just use it as an end of year social run.

The course is flat, along a windy seafront promenade, very congested at the start. I set off way too fast, 7minutes/km for the first 5 km. I have a condition called Raynaud's which means I have bad circulation in my hands and feet, so bad that they are almost always a different colour to the rest of my body, always cold even in the middle on the summer when the sun is out. This gets worse when exercising and even worse in the cold, and caused problems in this race. There were water stations but that was it, no other fuel, so at mid-point in the race when I went to get a gel, I couldn't feel my hands. It was so bad that I couldn't get hold of the gel, and having fumbled several times I realised that even if I did get hold of it I would either have dropped it or would have not been able to open it (this has happened before). I therefore had to run the second half with nothing more than water, again in those stupid flimsy cups in which water spills out every

I got through the second half by running side by side with a younger girl who was running for Winchester Running Club. She pulled me along up to the final mile, when I got my backside into gear and raced off towards the finishing line, overtaking several people in that final mile and picking up pace.

I ended this race in 1 hr. 34 mins, 372nd out of 1574 runners (there were loads of did not starters, maybe weather was an issue?), just one minute outside my own pb which was pretty good all things considered.  Amazingly I even reached 10 miles quicker than ever before, more on that in my next race. I celebrated by going to the local shops and buying myself a new camouflage buff – how cool do I look!?!?

Hayling 10 Sunday November 30th 2014

2 weeks after the Gosport half marathon, and at short notice, I entered this race. I saw this as another end of year wind-down, just 10 miles across varied surfaces but flat. Hayling Island is on my doorstep so no worries with travel, the entry fee was cheap, it seemed to be a fast race and most of the runners were club runners – possibly getting tuned up for the forthcoming cross country season.

I had continued with the faster running plan leading up to this, I must admit my shins were now hurting more and more so I was stretching those loads and taking pain killers. In hindsight I should have been resting, I know that now, but this was going to be my 11th race this year, my obsession with numbers was driving me towards a stupid target of 12 races in 12 months – well actually it would be 12 races in 11 months since the first was in February. I don't know if you have similar problems with numbers, I like whole numbers and will run past my house when returning back from a run to finish on a whole number; I also like playing games on a treadmill such as 5.00km in 20.00min. If I go past 20 mins or 5k then I will often continue to the next milestone. That's weird isn't it? It's not even just limited to running, I do it all the time, I loved maths and numbers at school, my favourite jobs were also linked to numbers.

Anyway, back to the race, it was a short fast race so I will keep this similar, short and fast. A bad mistake at the start, I didn't go for a pee, and the start line was in a residential street so no last minute bush peeing possible. There were a lot of runners all crowded together, the race start was called, and we were off. First few miles were fine, I felt good, apart from needing to pee. As we set off down a trail (the Hayling Billy Line), I eyed the bushes to either side and kept thinking "shall I, shan't I?" The more I thought about this, the more I needed to stop so I disappeared behind a bush, did my business and carried on. At the bottom of the trail we turned onto a road along the seafront, there was some nutter of a runner who was spending more energy shouting encouragement at other runners than he was running, I stayed with him for a while for a tow and then hooked up with another runner and we sped off. We chatted quite a lot at we went out along the seafront, unfortunately didn't get his name, but he helped me a lot at this point as I was losing interest in the run, perhaps it was because it was short and float, however the thought of a did not finish filled me we dread, so I carried on.

I remember saying to this guy that I always seem to do well in the first 75% of a race, and then struggle in the final 25%. This rule is true no matter what the distance, 5k all the way up to marathon distance. As an example, in the Gosport half I reached 75% point (10 miles) in a new 10 mile pb, but then I finished the final 3 miles slow just outside a half marathon pb. The same was happening in this 10 mile race, 7 miles flew by (apart from the pee break), but then I started struggling. The final 1km I got my motivation back, kicked on and, together with my running partner, cross the line in 1 hr. 11 mins, a little slower than my 10 mile point in the Gosport half. Placed

83rd out of 444, well inside the top 20%, the 26th non club runner out of 191.

At the end of the race I chatted to a few other people I knew, and then headed home. There wasn't really any feeling of achievement in this race, running 10 miles flat was no longer what I'd call pushing myself, I had to end the year fixing that.

Thames Run Ultra 50k Saturday December 13th 2014

So here it was, my final challenge for the year, another 50k race, something which would fix the comments from the last race about pushing myself, it would also achieve my 12 races in 12 months goal. I entered at short notice; it was a flat race along the river Thames, described as trail but probably more pavement. There was a limit of 100 runners, but not all for the ultra-distance – as you went along the route there were start points for ultra, marathon, half marathon and 10k races.

My shins were now worse than ever, so much so that I had to cut back my running a little, and then every now and again I'd push myself and run further. The weekend before the race I was a little worried so ran 20 miles on Saturday (which was hard), and then to prove to myself I can manage 30 miles I also ran 10 miles the next day early in the morning (felt really hard!). The week before the race I was working in Switzerland, flying home late on Friday, and the race was for some weird reason being run on a Saturday (most races are on Sundays), starting at 8am in Chertsey which is just over an hour drive away. This was not ideal preparation, but I had paid my entrance and so was committed to running it.

I also encouraged two other friends to enter, both were experienced Ultra runners. One of them (Jacob) pulled out at the last minute through an injury (far more sensible than me); the other (Alan) had an injury but was stupid like me and ran it (despite turning up 10 minutes late at the start).

While working in Switzerland I did a really sensible taper, Monday I started on 5 miles and then dropped a mile every day until Friday which was 1 mile. I also stuck to a reasonable diet despite Xmas festivities going on, no alcohol, minimal junk food, etc. I was trying to ensure I did everything I could do in order to finish this race; all was going perfect apart from my sore shin.

One thing I couldn't plan for was the flight home, disaster struck when I got to Zurich airport; all flights in and out of the UK were cancelled due to an air traffic control computer failure. When I learnt about this I thought it was fate telling me I shouldn't enter the race, I was already due to get home at 10:30pm, giving me minimal sleep before the race, so was this a force from above giving me a sign ? I waited and waited at the airport, half hoping I wouldn't get home that night, but eventually I got on the very last flight which was due to leave at 10:30pm (airspace closes after that). Eventually I got home at 01:30am, enough time for about 3.5 hours of sleep before heading off for the race – crazy, stupid, mad, stubborn.

Sally was going to do her first marshalling role at this race so she came up with me; it was well below freezing and pitch black. She waved me off as about 20 of us started the race at the start line, amazingly I felt pretty good at the start, and perhaps the freezing weather had numbed the pain in my shin?

I was chatting away, sticking quite easily with the front runners, when early in the race, probably less than a couple of miles in, we moved from the river edge up onto a main road, I remember stubbing my foot against the river bank. When I did this I stumbled forward, the numbness disappearing and quickly replaced by what felt like a shockwave through my foot, leg, and into my right buttock cheek. I felt pain but then it went, either replaced by the cold weather numbing the pain or adrenalin.

The race continued at quite a social pace, checkpoints every 5 miles kept us fed well, the course was pretty well marked apart from at one point when we couldn't agree which was the right or the wrong route and split into 2 – luckily I chose to follow a stranger who knew the area rather than friends who didn't.

As the sun came up and the weather warmed at about mile 16, I began to get more aware of a pain in my right leg, which then turned into a slight limp. This was annoying as I'd done pretty well in the race, sticking with the leading pack quite easily, maybe even in with a chance of a decent finishing position. We had got to 21 miles in around 2h45m, possibly the easiest and fastest I'd ever done this, but the limp was getting worse. I approached a checkpoint and the race organiser, Carlos, asked if I was okay. Stubborn me replied "yes, I will be fine but I may have to walk a little to finish it". I carried on and then disaster struck, the limp became really painful; I decided to stretch and walk. I walked for a mile, it took me 13 minutes, then I went another in 14 minutes, then a final mile in over 15 minutes, the mental strength had tried to overcome the physical (lack of) strength, this had served me well all year, but now it was having the opposite effect and damaging my body. I was stumbling along a tow path, on my own, in so much pain, and felt like crying. A did not finish was on the cards, damage to my leg was definitely on the cards, and I'd let down Sally, friends and family by failing. I collapsed on the pavement in Richmond, phoned Sally to apologise whilst holding back the tears, and then spoke to Carlos who got someone to pick me up. I'd reached 24 miles in 3hr 40 minutes.

I was transported onto the finish line and then carried out of the car, not able to put any pressure on my right leg. Sally fed and watered me, then got me up to the changing room where I showered and changed. I dumped my trainers and hydration pack in a bin, in my mind they were now cursed, and then went back outside to sit with my friends. Ultra runners are mostly a friendly bunch, there are a few prima donnas who think they are above all others, but 99.9% are great, I always make new friends in these circles either at races or through social media. Alan had now crossed the finishing line but was also worse for wear, another stubborn person but with a lot more to lose than me as he was training for the Marathon des Sables in April 2015.

I was in no rush to head home, to be honest I couldn't even imagine how I'd get back to the car which was parked back at the start line 50km away, so we headed to the pub for a drink. 3 pints later and my leg was feeling better, maybe it was the drink as I had not drunk 3 pints in one go all year. Sally, Alan and I headed off to the train station at 4pm, plenty of time to avoid the football fans from the nearby Chelsea stadium where the match was ending at 4:45pm. Unfortunately this wasn't quite the case since as soon as I started walking I realised the damaged leg was now even worse, we got to Fulham Broadway station at the same time as 40,000 football fans arrived.

Eventually we made it back to the car, Sally drove me home, and I collapsed on the floor, emotionally and physically drained. My first ever did not finish, not because I couldn't run 50k but because I'd injured myself.

## Training

I've got to the end of this book and realised I've not mentioned too much about my training.

When I was bodybuilding I initially made the mistake of buying magazines and then following the programmes written in them, expecting to grow and become famous like those in the pictures.

It didn't work out like this, I struggled for time, I over trained, I didn't grow, but I did gain experience through reading, experimenting, and learning.

This is what I now do with my running, I read magazines and search the web, I find programmes which I like, and I adopt them to suit my preferences, lifestyle, and ability.

I've mentioned the FIRST schedule, this is a great 3 day programme, but the speeds don't suit my running style – I'm not that fast. So I took the programme, adapted it, and when I started increasing distances, say from 26 mile to 30 mile, I took the FIRST programme and added on 10 to 20% to the distances. This resulted in me sticking to my marathon schedule with a slight adaption, rather than finding a new ultra marathon schedule.

I'm now on a new schedule, the reason I switched is because of my love of hills, and this programme has them most weeks. I currently can't run but I can do the same schedule on a bike (take the distance to run and double it, or work out how long the distance would take if I were running and aim for same time), and as I recover I can do some days on the cross trainer. Hopefully as my recovery continues I can do one or two of the short days running and then gradually build up.

So in summary, read, listen, take in information, even join some groups on Facebook, and then listen to your body and adapt the programme to suit you. You are the only person who can listen directly to your body, it gives you early warning signals (such as the plantar and shin splint issues I had), just make sure you listen to them (just as I didn't).

What next?

I was unable to move off the floor for several days after that, literally sat on my backside sliding around on our wooden floor. I contemplated so much while sat there, was a did not finish better than a did not start (possible answer was "no" given the outcome, unfortunately my love of quotes such as "better to try and fail rather than not try at all" makes me ignore such signs), would I have finished the race (yes, definitely), what did people now think of me now I was a failure (feeling sorry for myself at this point), what next?

The "what next" question was a dilemma, I hate doctors but I knew I was in trouble. I thought I'd learnt my lesson from the blood poisoning episode when bodybuilding, but I still decided to sit at home, raising my leg, icing it, compressing it, whilst also Googling my symptoms and trying everything I could to get better. Xmas came and went, I was unable to leave the house but luckily I was able to mostly work from home plus had taken Xmas and New Year as holiday so did not ruin my record of no sick days in 10 years. After Xmas I decided to get to the doctors.

The UK NHS is great up to a point, but you do feel like an item in a production line sometimes. I visited the doctor, explained what had happened, and was prescribed rest and pain killers – it was almost like they were looking at the same Google pages as I had been. I asked about physio but was told I'd be waiting at least 18 weeks for this; my injury will probably have cleared up by then. Luckily I also have private health insurance through work so phoned them up, within a few days I was at a physio who checked me out and diagnosed a hairline fracture in my shin, damaged hip and sprained knee. The NHS told me I was limping because of the damage to my lower leg, the private physio diagnosed a worsening damaged lower leg due to my right hip being knocked out of alignment, and it was literally higher than my left hip. Cause and effect, get to know the difference!

7 physio appointments later brings me to the end of this story, my hip is now straightened, I'm limping less and the pain in my shin and knee is reducing. I have been able to get on a bike and cycle I've even recently got on the cross trainer and simulated running, but 51 days after injuring myself I still can only dream of running. I go for an MRI scan soon to check my cruciate ligament; they think this may be damaged so I may be waiting a little longer before I can say I'm well on the road to recovery.

I've done a few things to keep me motivated, I've entered a few races (May, 3 Forts 27 mile, 500m elevation, and August, Peak District Sky Race, 30 miles, 2000m elevation, plus a cheeky little 50 miler in Wales in November) with the goal of continuing my quest to challenge myself, not only run further, but also harder and higher (love those hills more and more), and to visit new places while meeting some great new people. All of these races would have been beyond me in 2014, at the moment they are still beyond me, but I love setting myself a challenge and then working out how I can achieve it – I think far too many people worry too much about the journey, then convince themselves to give up on the goal. With age comes experience, with experience comes risk aversion, with risk aversion comes lost opportunities – I challenge this was of thinking all the time. I may not make either of these races, who knows, but I have nothing to lose apart from an entry fee which will go to a good cause if I fail to make the start line.

I've enjoyed the cycling so have entered a 50 mile bike race in Salisbury in May. I'll definitely manage to do this, perhaps not fast, but I've done 30 + miles in recent weeks so it won't be a problem unless the MRI scans show I need surgery on my knee.

## Ending

So that's it, my first year of racing, and a year after taking up running. In my first year I covered around 2,000km, in my second year I covered around 2,000 miles, perhaps quantity over quality?

I've learnt a lot in this year, about my mind, my body, and my limitations. I will use my mind to listen to my body in future, as opposed to using it to overcome the signs my body is giving me.

I have met and been inspired by a lot of cool people this year, I want to be like them and then become the same, an inspiration to others. I want to take this into my day job, to do the very best I can for my manager who has put a lot of trust in me, and to inspire people to challenge the status quo not just in their lives but also in their work.

At the end of the year in a call with my boss she said something which makes this year, including the injury, feel so worthwhile. She told me that both she and others had noticed a change in me, a change for the better. She said I'd become more relaxed, happier, and nicer to be around. I told her that this had always been my goal in and out of work, if you are in a state like this then people find you more approachable, want to work with you, and then together you deliver better results. My job isn't to tell people they aren't working well and how to do things better, I'm there to help people see these themselves and inspire them to improve – they know this already, they just don't always see it.

What happens in 2015, I don't know right now. I have good and bad days, I would be disappointed if I don't get to do the races I've entered but it won't be the end of the world, there are other hobby's out there waiting to be experienced. I'm trying everything to get better, diet, rehab, even rubbing my Buddha's belly. For now I will just be content with walking pain free in the fresh winter air, across the South Downs National Park, with my wife.

I hope you've enjoyed reading this as much as I enjoyed 2014 and that it's inspired you, at least a little, to challenge yourself to do something different. If you want to get in touch with me email markcameron666@gmail.com or search me on social networking sites (Facebook, Twitter, Instagram, LinkedIn), I'm easy to find.

All the best

Mark

**Book 2: The Average Runner**

**This book is dedicated to all the people that have helped me get to where I am today; I wouldn't have got this far without you, thank you.**

**Regards,**

# If you want to run far, go together

**Mark Cameron (the average runner)**

Chapter Title



Appendix



Please note due to the huge variety of devices on which you can view Amazon books, formatting this book to fit all sizes has proved a task probably as big as actually writing the words. If I'd known in advance of this I may have reconsidered making it longer than the last book and taken out all photographs, but I decided to do my best and keep the book as intended. If I could give anyone thinking of writing a Kindle book, I'd say keep it simple!

## Introduction

In February 2015 I published my first book, initially I found the need to write it solely for personal gain, I was injured, feeling low, and needed to pick myself up. While I wrote the book and recalled some great moments, I realised my year (2014) had not been as bad as it first seemed, one bad moment does make a bad year, and decided to use the book to say thank you to those who had helped make it so great. I also wanted it to be inspiring to others to look at life in this way, to challenge themselves to do something new, and maybe even to have a laugh as they saw some of what I had written in them.

I think the book achieved all this, for me and others. Surprisingly it was downloaded over 4,000 times in around 9 months, I had some really nice emails and social media contacts from people who had read it, and it remains hanging around the top 10 in many of the Amazon charts despite me making no effort to publicise it now. I gave the book away for free as often as I was allowed to by Amazon; it was made available for free on Kindle Unlimited, and when I had to put a unit price on it I set the lowest allowable price of 99 pence so it was something anyone could afford. The royalties I received, which were not much since I signed up for the lowest possible royalty rate so I could set such low/zero prices, were used to enter the races in 2015 and give to the charities supported in those races.

I have written this book for less personal reasons than before, I'm in pretty good shape all things considered, but I still wanted to give thanks to those people who have made 2015 a pretty awesome year. I used the title "If you want to run far, run together" because of this, it's running with people, meeting people in person, and forming what I would call a more "real" circle of friends (less virtual friends), that was a goal and now has been a highlight for me this year. I have extensively used photographs because I like photographs when I read other books. They say a picture can speak a thousand words; I shudder to think how long this book would have ended up being if I hadn't used so many photos.

I do hope you enjoy reading this book as much as I enjoyed the events which lead to me writing this book, if you do then please leave a review on Amazon and feel free to get in contact with me (markcameron@gmail.com). If you didn't enjoy it, I'd love to know why, I'm not scared of feedback as it's what my day job involves every day, I'm not pretending this is a masterpiece, and I appreciate I can't please everyone.

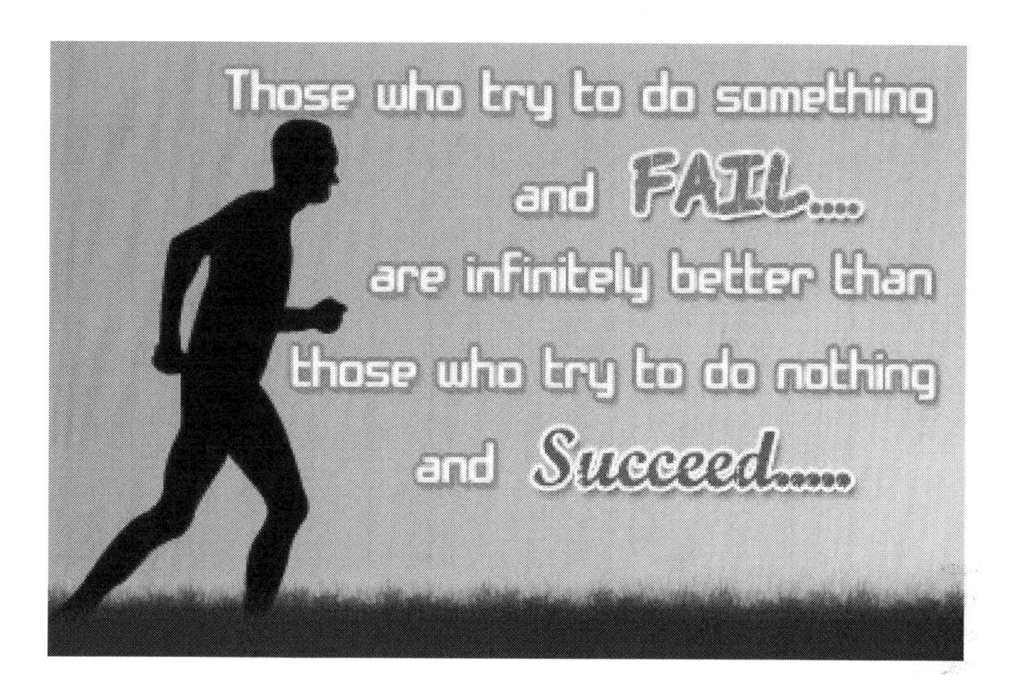
Those who try to do something
and FAIL....
are infinitely better than
those who try to do nothing
and Succeed.....

## I'm injured, so let's enter some races

So 2014 ended on a low, I injured myself, and as a result suffered my first DNF which to me felt like total failure. I started feeling sorry for myself, my leg was in a really bad shape, I couldn't even stand up and was dragging myself along the floor around the house, but I still took things really personally and this began spiralling in a downwards direction, a feeling I had experienced a few times in the past. Because of previous experiences, I acknowledge these feeling and decided to pick myself back up by taking the following actions:

- Writing my book
- Entering more races in 2015
- Buying running more running gear
- Using forums to keep myself motivated
- Cycling

It's funny how when you can't do something you enjoy; you try to do more of it. I couldn't even walk for more than 100 metres until March, yet there I was searching the internet, finding races that were longer and higher than I'd completed in 2014.

Races I ended up entering were based on my chosen purpose for running. Last year was my first year of racing and got carried away with quantity. I just wanted to run as many races as possible, maybe meet new people, to enjoy the experience of taking part in events (something I'd missed since bodybuilding, the thrill of the day), and visit some new places. I say new places in the loosest possible way, almost all my races were within an hour drive of home, but it's amazing how these races take you along routes that are on your doorstep, yet you've never know existing.

Challenging the status quo is so important to me so I looked at this purpose, and challenged it. I was happy with what I'd achieved, but still wanted to get something more from running. I'd looked at pictures of people on the internet and in magazines running in some awesome locations, in the UK and abroad. The names of these places I'd heard of, but if you gave me a map I wouldn't be able to locate them (even the UK ones), so I decided to focus on visiting some of these places in 2015 via running, I was going to stretch my boundaries further than the hour drive of 2014.

So while sat on the floor, searching the internet, I entered the following races

- May 2015 Three Forts Challenge – 1,000 metres of ascent, 27.2 miles, across the South Downs. I always say I won't enter the same race twice, I have absolutely no interest in trying to beat last years' time, and yet I'd entered this in 2014. Difference is I entered the half marathon last year, which had much less elevation, plus it was a good stepping stone towards future races. The challenge here is about just getting to the start line, and then crawling over the finish line. I knew I'd have very little time to get ready, but completing it was to be the goal. Even better for me on this race was getting someone I'd met online (not one of those online sites!) to meet and run – Jacob Adamiec (see photo). I think Jacob is Polish, I've never actually asked him, but he's a really nice guy. He runs what appears to be an effortless 50km almost every Sunday just for training, he is also a great photographer and has many photos of some awesome places, the kind of places which I referred to as inspiring me to keep pushing my boundaries for exploring.

- June 2015 Three Peaks Challenge – this is not really a race, more of a hike. Climb the 3 highest peaks in Scotland, England, and Wales, ideally within 24hrs. The challenge here is as much about getting from country to country (by road) as climbing the mountains. This event was arranged by the person who arranged the event I injured myself in 2014, so fingers crossed lightening won't strike twice. Again, this event has a purpose, it's all about elevation, something I challenged myself with in 2014 and will do again in 2015, plus seeing places in the UK that I'd never have done without this event
- August 2015 Peak Sky Run – I listened to other runners and wanted an ace race to do. I'd seen adverts and articles on Sky Running, it looked awesome, so I couldn't believe my luck when I saw a webpage for this event, some amazing photographs of the locations, an awesome looking elevation profile, and it actually allowed me to enter – no questions asked! I entered without thinking, then reality sunk in – first things first, where on earth is the Peak District, what does 2,000m elevation equate to ?
- November 2015 Brecon Beacon Ultra – Sat in front of the TV one night, a "friend" (Rich Knowles) popped up on messenger on my tablet and asked if I wanted to enter this. He sent me a link, I thought to myself if I say no I'd look weak, I didn't have time to ponder as the race fills up quick plus I could pay via PayPal – so I simply entered, in seconds it was done. I hadn't even checked the distance (50 miles), elevation, terrain, and had no idea where Brecon was (it's an are in Wales used as an SAS training ground). This one scared me a bit, too many unknowns, but Rich agreed to drive so I was looking at it like a jolly boys outing

2015

New year.
New people.
New things.
New happiness.
New disappointments.
New chances.

I also entered a backup race, just in case I fail to get running again, this would be my first bike race – 50 miles in May, 2 weeks after the Three Forts. I was 100% sure this would be within my capabilities, I'd cycled 50 miles during rehab, it was in Salisbury in the UK which was fairly local, and was in aid of the Samaritans which is a good cause.

Despite the best efforts of others to encourage me to enter further races, I stopped at that, no more races entered while I was injured. I was proud I'd moved from quantity to something more strategic, just as I was trying to do at work. Each race was planned so it had a purpose which leads to the goal of completing the Peak Sky Race, the Brecon race will be a celebration of the year and preparation for trying new things in 2016.

Now all I had to do was to get walking, and then running, again, how hard can that be?

## Rehab, what a pain

Apart from the bloody poisoning I contracted while bodybuilding, I don't remember ever having a serious injury. I've played rugby, I've lifted heavy weights, I've had a few altercations while working clubs and bars, but never had anything major happen to me, so with this lack of experience, along with what I call my biggest strength "impatience" (at work I'm told it's a weakness, but impatience leads to getting things done, so how is that weak?), rehab was going to be rushed through but inevitably take twice as long. My calf was so tight at this time; it was permanently tense and painful.

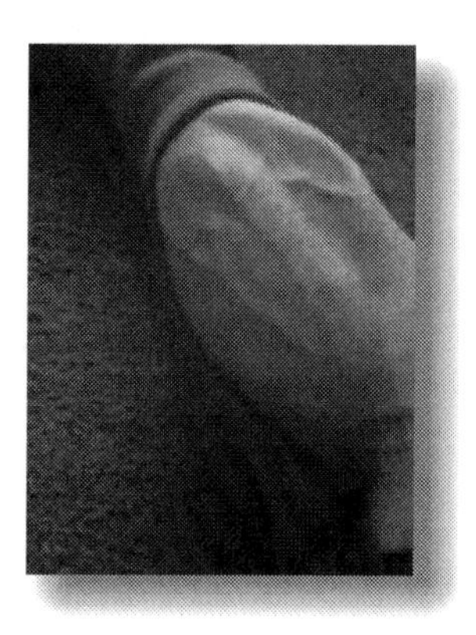

When I injured myself, rather than go straight to the doctors I took the sensible option of making sure I enjoyed Christmas and New Year, taking lots of pills, resting up at home, and trying all kinds of remedies to magic myself better. My calf was so tight, my knee felt like it would buckle under me at any point, but I'm so stubborn I continued to ignore things. As expected, by the time the New Year had gone, around 4 weeks later, I could still barely walk, so rather than go to the doctors I took the wise decision to work in Switzerland – I was amazed they let me on the plane, I thought they'd offer me wheelchair assistance as I hobbled around Heathrow airport. Needless to say this stubbornness backfired massively, the trip was great, well worth it from a business perspective, and I did manage to fool myself into thinking it was doing me good thanks to the ice-bath they had in the hotel gym (15 minutes stood in there and I couldn't feel a thing after), but by the time I hobbled from the taxi back to my front door I knew I'd done more damage. I'm so stupid sometimes, this was probably the worst decision I'd make in this rehab period as it would set me back weeks.

I gave into the nagging from various people and booked in for a doctor's appointment. I don't go to the doctors, hadn't been for ages, and had heard horror stories of the problems getting appointments. For my doctors I found out I can do this via an app. on my tablet, the health service had evolved since I'd last visited, so I searched for a suitable day and time, chose a doctor, then clicked on "book appointment" and it was done, so simple. Unfortunately the time slots are just 10 minutes long, so when I turned up and explained what had happened, I felt like I was on the kind of production line which my Lean/Continuous Improvement work head so often criticizes. I was told I'd sprained my knee and to take ibuprofen, ice my leg, and elevate it (so the standard RICE procedure which I had already been doing). It's a shame that such a clever doctor who had spent years learning her trade was no doubt rushed into making such an amazing suggestion by the stupid productivity targets some guru consultant has thought up as a result of some productivity review. Please shoot me if I ever get like that in my project role.

Being a little unhappy with this advice I had two options to get a second opinion:

1) Go onto Facebook, put a post on a Group page outlining (in my expert opinion) what is wrong with me and asking complete strangers for advice, then trawl the responses until I get one I like
2) Probably a better option, lucky for me I also get BUPA cover through work, I've been there 10 years and never used it, but I could consider using them (free)

I was desperate but also sensible so I chose option two, it wasn't the first one which came to mind but I it was a work benefit I had never used, instead of asking for more benefits why not use what I already have?

The process was amazing, I phoned them up, they approved treatment immediately and offered me options of where to go for a consultation, I picked one and within a few days I was being seen to by a local physio named Gary Sadler, who had worked with several Premier League football clubs He diagnosed I'd actually damaged my hip, as well as my knee and shin, but without fixing the hip the other two would not heal (he was doing root cause analysis, treat the cause, not the symptoms, as usual I was linking this back to my day job – a great way to link practice back to theory). My right hip had slipped from the impact of jarring my leg, which caused me to limp, meaning I ran awkward and further damaged the knee and shin, my right hip was now higher than my left. Apparently most people have this imbalance, it's something you get used to, but when running for many miles, with a huge difference and already damaged legs, the results are much worse. I love understanding things, not just being told, as it makes life so much more interesting, and having heard Gary's explanation I started asking more questions, thinking about how I could make things better long term (laptop rucksack, always heavy as it's my mobile office, only ever carry it on one shoulder, causing my hips to slip), and looking for examples while I was out and about (women, be aware of those massive handbags you seem to carry with one arm at a 90 degree angle, you're causing an imbalance in your posture).

I would spend the next 2 months going to the physio once or twice a week to slowly move my hip back into place. Each time it would move in the right direction, and then slip back a little again, but for the short term it was helping. I was also doing some new hip strengthening exercises using resistance bands at home and also replaced my desk chair in my home office with a Swiss ball to sit on, both of which were helping me improve myself for the long term. I was able to get fresh air and more active by cycling, my bike had been sat around doing nothing since completing the Strava Grand Fondo challenge last year, and grew to like this so much which resulted in me entering the Sam's ride Sportive. Here's a photo of me setting off for a cycle ride while injured, you can clearly see the limp/lean.

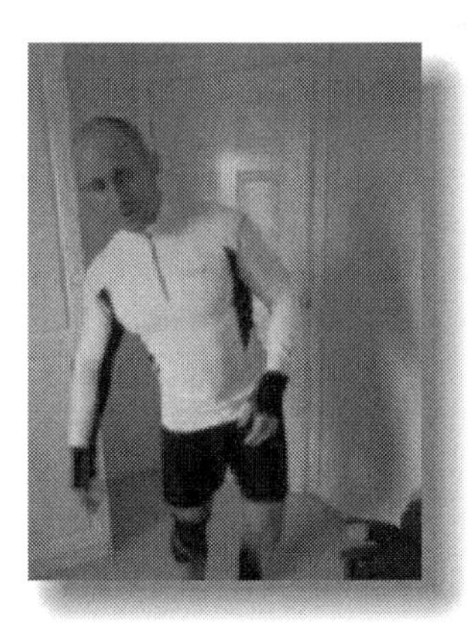

It got to March and my hip was getting stronger all the time. I told Gary that I still felt my knee and shin recovery were lagging a lot, obviously this had nothing to do with the healing process taking longer due to my age (I was still young at 42, that's young isn't it?), he assured me things would improve if I gave it time but agreed to send me off for an MRI scan.

I had no idea what to expect with an MRI, but thanks to BUPA I was in a private hospital within a week and getting this done. I amazed the nurses by sleeping all the way through the scan, I called it meditating but I think you need to be semiconscious to mediate, I was definitely fully asleep throughout, not aware of what was going on until the machine stopped and the nurses woke me up. I got the results through shortly after, the consultant gave me some great news, not only had I not got any major cruciate damage, but my knee was also in a much better than expected for someone of my age and history of sport – whoever tells you heavy squats are bad for you is lying, I think it's more to do with using bad form for squats or any other activity, that cause the damage.

Buoyed by this news, I decided to focus my mind on thinking myself better. I had about 16 weeks until the Three Forts Challenge in May and decided I was in with a shout of doing it. I still could barely walk 100 metres, but I could cycle for miles and had my training plan ready (it was an "advanced" plan for sub 3 hour runners!). That cliché "think outside the box" came to mind, so I decided to do my running plan on my bike, plus I could use the gym bike if the weather wasn't so good. I also observed I knew many great cyclists who were occasional runners, but also were pretty good runners, so I set off and started my marathon running training plan, on my bike.

Gary stepped up the rehab, sometimes attaching electrical currents to my leg and leaving me to watch the muscles in my leg twitch about in all funny ways. I was also getting better with core strength, I could stand on my bad leg longer and longer (in discomfort) and could sit on the Swiss ball with both feet off the ground and balance. When I said previously "I would think myself better" that was no joke, I'd read books on this before, a positive attitude can drag you up, just as a negative one can drag you down (which I was in danger of before writing my first book).

As my leg healed more and more, I started walking further and further. Let's call it interval training, or the walking version of the run/walk strategy. I'd walk a little, then sit down, then walk a little further, similar to how I see pensioners walk around in the high street. I did hill reps by walking (as opposed to crawling) up the stairs, and then started to progress to walking and down the hill at the end of my road. This was one memorable walk early in the morning before work, took ages, felt great.

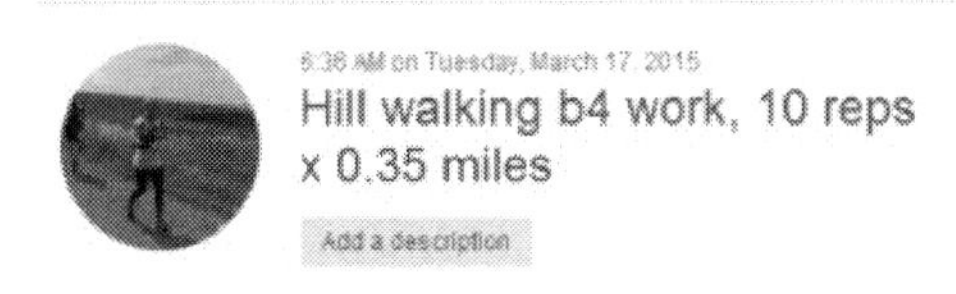


| 11.6km | 1:41:22 | 8:43/km |
|---|---|---|
| Distance | Moving Time | Pace |

| Elevation | 308m | Calories | 1,143 |
|---|---|---|---|
| Elapsed Time | 1:42:36 | | |

Device: Garmin Forerunner 220

I had also been swimming, wish I'd started that a long time ago as put no pressure on my leg but doing breast stroke gave my knee a good workout, and then as things progressed I also got onto the elliptical trainer in the gym to at least simulate a running movement.

Beginning of April the good news came, Gary said I could start jogging again, I knew long runs would be out of the question, so too would speed training, but if I just focussed on getting some time on my feet and didn't care about finishing time at the Three Forts then I knew, with about 4 weeks to go, I was in with a shout.

So totally ignoring advice, I set off like an idiot, 8k my first run back (slowly), then 13, then 16, and within 2 weeks I'd done 22km in one go, all done very slow though with plenty of rest periods. I was still going to physio, I'd be asked how my jogging was going, I'd respond and say "fine", he never asked how far I'd ran and I so strictly speaking I never lied to him. The pain was still there in my shin every time I stepped on it, I was not able to hop on the bad leg as I'd simply collapse on the floor when I landed, I was told a lot of this could be bone bruising since the MRI showed nothing mechanical was wrong with the knee and the small fracture in my shin was definitely healing, so there was light at the end of the tunnel.

I know in hindsight I could have done more to get better quicker, I could have got myself signed off work for months and sat on my backside resting, I could have been more patient and listened to Gary more, but I took the hard route – well it was hard on my body, but I think it was the best route for my mind.

The rest of training went well, gradually increase the volume of running and reducing the cycling, I think I did around 14 runs in total for this race, physically I was aware I wasn't strong but mentally I was well up for the challenge of the race.

The week leading up to the race I did a proper taper the week before to ensure I gave myself every chance I completing it, plenty of rest and stretching.

I felt pressure due at least turn up on the day and give it a go. I had Jacob coming and didn't want to miss the chance to meet him. I think it was his first race in the UK so I wanted to be part of this day with him.

Next chapter is the comeback race, I'd be there on the start line, battered but wiser than ever before, plus would be meeting Jacob.................

EVERY SETBACK IS A
SETUP FOR AN EVEN
GREATER COMEBACK

## The comeback – Three Forts Challenge (03/05)

I did the half marathon last year for this event, I've always said I will never do the same (except Parkrun) race twice but I am happy to do the same event at a different distance, hence me being here. Sticking to the strict definition of an ultra, this is an ultra as the event is longer than a marathon but only by one extra mile.

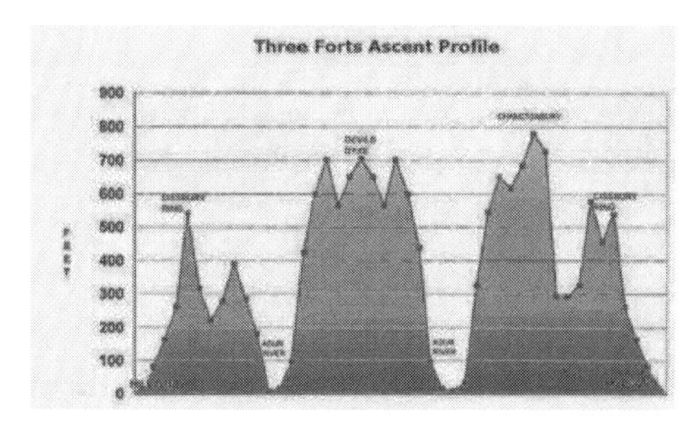


We could write an entire chapter, maybe even a book, on what makes a race an ultra, not a week goes past when you don't see the question raised and argued over on a Facebook forum, so I'm not going to get dragged into this in much detail. All I will say on the subject is strictly speaking anything more than a marathon in length is an ultra (check the entry on Wikipedia), this could be 27.2 miles (as this one is) or, as many would say the definition should be, could be the classic distances on 50km upwards. Comparing my first 50km Ultra race, which was on a totally flat course along a canal and that people were happy to call an ultra-marathon, to this one which was 27.2 miles across a very hilly South Downs (which is a national park on the South Coast of the UK), I know which I feel is more worthy of being called an Ultra and is far more testing.

I do think some people get a little snobby as they move up the distances, someone who completes a 50 mile race may look down on shorter 50k races, only to then be looked down themselves by those who complete 100 mile and more races. I admire all who give any distance a go and push themselves, I think they are awesome for even giving it a go, and a huge kudos to those who push themselves harder by running further and higher than before, but challenging your own limits should not mean forgetting where you came from and trying to move the goal posts for others.

I don't know why they call this race "Challenge" rather than "Ultra" – are they ashamed it's a short ultra, do they not want to be dragged into this pointless debate over titles ? It's a great race, in a great location, and I reckon tagging it with the word Ultra will only increase its popularity.

Anyway, back to the race.

As mentioned earlier, this was the race where I'd get to meet one of my online friends, Jacob, as well as meeting his wife, Vicky, who I'm pretty sure is from Peru, unfortunately for her I met her at the end of the race when I was in not fit state to move or talk, I'd get to meet her properly at a later race.

As a bonus, I also got to meet another contact, Stephen Cousins, at the start line. For those of you who haven't heard of Stephen then look him up, he's known for a number of things: photography (weddings), video's (filmmyrun.com / YouTube channel), and also rock star (ever heard of "John Ketley is a weatherman" or the group "A Tribe of Toffs" ?).

Stephen was easy to spot at the start line with his Go-Pro, doing the intro to his latest video, so I interrupted him and had a chat. The thing that amazes me is that Stephen knocks out really good times across many distances, times I can only dream of, and somehow manages to do this while making really cool films. Stephen overtook me early on in the race, because he's a nice guy he slowed down to chat, allowing me a guest appearance in his race video, and then he was gone, I didn't see him again all race.

The day came, the weather was shocking (last year it was shorts and vest weather, this year it was rain jacket, gloves and running tights), and I considered using this as a really lame excuse to pull out.

Thankfully Jacob had been in touch, he was staying local and looking forward to it, so no time for excuses - Sally and I set off early in the morning and headed to the race venue.

Having been there before I knew it would be well organised so we left it late, I registered, got myself ready, and looked around for Jacob. He found me at the start line, there I was dressed as if it were winter, with my new Innov8 ultra vest on, and there he was in shorts and T-shirt, I think it was obvious which of us was planning on finishing the race quickest !

The race started, Jacob set off into the distance and I wouldn't see him again until the end of the race, I religiously stuck to my game plan of running slowly and just getting around. I've said in the past I like running trails as enjoying the views, well here is an image from last year

And this is the reality of this year

It was raining, foggy, muddy, and windy, I couldn't see a thing, and for the entire race I kept talking to myself asking why the hell I was there. It was horrid, and to make matters worse I was chugging along at such a slow pace I had even more time than usual to ~~enjoy~~ hate it.

I don't remember much about this race apart from the weather, and the great marshals – moaning about myself being cold and wet seems terrible, they had to stay out there even longer.

Bad choice of shoes last year ruined my feet, this year I was a little wiser, I also wore a shower proof jacket plus my new Innov8 ultra vest. If I could run the race again I would not have bothered with the jacket, the only good thing about it was I had 2 extra pockets to store things, but it was a pain to run it, showerproof does not mean rainproof, I still got soaked but with the jacket I also got way too hot. The ultra-vest was a treat to me for the race; I chose that particular one so I could have 2 bottles on the chest straps plus the water bladder as back up on my back. Last year I ran with a vest with just a bladder, problem was that by having the liquid hidden on my back I was never really aware of how much I was drinking, I didn't have the experience to go by how I felt while running, and usually ended the race with loads of fluid left despite it being just a 2 litre bladder. With 500 ml bottles on each shoulder I could easily see and hear how much I was / wasn't drinking, one bottle per hour is how I planned things using this.

Stephen ran with me for a while, filming as he went, making things look really easy and chatting with myself and others. He eventually went off ahead of me, I then picked off other runners who ran up alongside me and chatted to them for as long as they'd listen, I was going so slow it was pretty easy to speak and run at the same time, one of the bonuses for slowing down.

I remember one event was at 18 miles, running up a hill with not the slightest hint of sun or warmth, but plenty of rain, I still got dehydrated and collapsed on the floor with cramp. Some kind runner stopped to ask if I was ok, as usual I put on a brave face and said yes, got up and started walking. I took in some electrolyte drink and later took in some salt tablets, but I still had cramp and had to start walking. My walk was not much slower than my running speed so it made very little difference overall I guess, I felt a fraud to walk so much but then again, lots of people around me were also walking, very few overtook me, instead of being in the top part of the field like last year, I was now in the middle or even back part of the pack where run/walk strategy was more common. I totally admire those who do this as I did consider on more than one occasion to pull out, nothing to do with the strategy, more to do with the fact it was taking ages and I'm really impatient. I was also feeling sorry for Sally, Jacob and Vicky who I hoped would be waiting at the finish line for me, but little did they know they would be waiting a lot longer than expected.

I ground out the final 9 miles, sometimes trying to run but quickly giving up as the cold and damp were now also hurting my sore leg, and then in the final km which was all downhill I thought I'd go with the grandstand finish and run. This lasted all of about 10 steps, I cramped, slipped, landed on the floor, and got overtaken by others as I tried to muster up enough strength to at least look partly happy as I crossed the line in 4 hrs 57 minutes, 171st out of 332 runners, all things considered it wasn't so bad.

Jacob, his wife (Vicky), and Sally were all waiting for me, I felt so guilty I'd kept them waiting, but felt so proud I'd completed this having only done so few runs in training for it. It was an ultra, the distance was more than a marathon and certainly tougher than many 50k's that other runners are happy to call ultra's, plus I'd overcome so much mentally and physically to finish this. Making it even more special was to hear Jacob had finished in 3rd place in 3 hr 30 minutes, I was glad he'd waited an hour and a half more in the rain to meet up with me after, double kudos for that. I had the most awful cramp after the race, they may have waited a while for me to finish but they had to wait almost as long for me to get out of my clothes and change into some clean clothes, it was one last episode of agony for the day.

I felt so strong mentally after finishing this race, yes my body was battered, I was soaking wet, slower than ever before, but I knew as I'd managed to complete this then the Peak District race was definitely still possible.

Key learning from this experience, when you have a goal you believe in, but the road to reach it appears blocked with obstacles, look for other routes – there's always a way. I followed this with the training, I couldn't run, I couldn't walk, but I could cycle.

The strongest
people aren't
always the people
who win,
but the people
who don't give up
when they lose

## The one where I got lost, my first sportive – Sam's Ride (17/05)

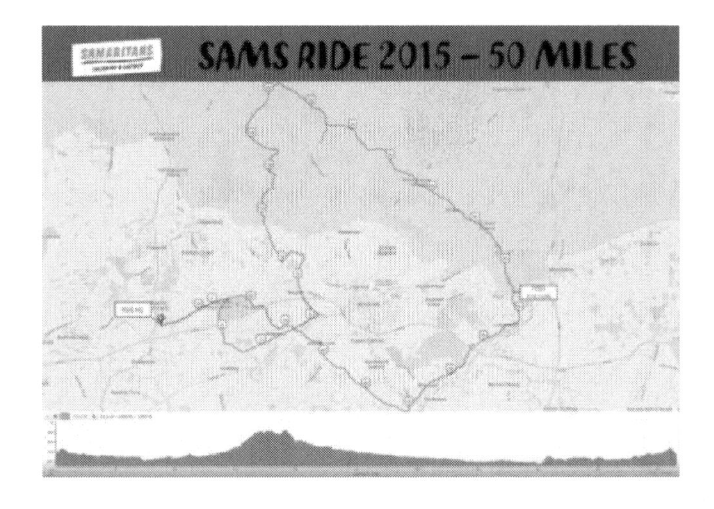


As I mentioned earlier, for rehab I got on my bike and rode miles and miles. I had never owned a road bike until August last year when I bought one due to making a stupid decision to enter a Strava ride challenge. I really enjoyed the fact I could cover relatively long distances in a fairly quick time (possibly I link to my impatience); usually out early on a Sunday when there were less idiots around on the roads.

My bike is not great, it's a bit of a tank, but for a guy who's relatively heavy, and very inexperienced, I think it's the right choice for now. I don't really ride it much different to my mountain bike which has fat tyres and suspension, by this I mean I go up and down kerbs without slowing down, I don't worry so much about avoiding potholes and drains, this bike has taken a battering but doesn't let me down – I've not even had a puncture !

Sam's Ride was my backup plan for the Three Forts, but despite achieving completing that foot race I decided to continue with the cycle option as well. The race was in aid of the Samaritans, something which I felt was a good cause based on my experience at the start of the injury.

For those who aren't aware, a Sportive is a non-competitive bike race, it's not on roads closed to the public so can't be classed as a race, they don't always have chip timings or finishing time goals. This one had a number of different distance options, you didn't even need a road bike to take part, and there were people of all ages there, even some on mountain bikes taking part.

I didn't know what to expect, I'd never been to this area, so we turned up early, registered, and then I got my bike ready. When running I pay very little attention to people's trainers, I don't believe saving a few ounces with super trainers will make that much difference to a runner who can probably achieve far more benefit saving a few kg's of bodyweight. At work I talk about our "sphere of influence" a lot which means don't look blame external factors like your tools or your products, instead take a look at yourself, there are always things we can do which are much more within our sphere of influence, but we often find it harder to look internally. At this event I must admit I paid more attention to all the super bikes that were around me, you see these cyclists out of the roads at the weekends and they look so professional in their club colours and smart bikes, I felt like I looked like a pick and mix sweet collection, nothing really matched. It's a dangerous thing cycling, easy to get green with envy and start trading up parts and then finally bite the bullet and get a new bike, I imagine costs can escalate very quickly, even more than with running where it's usually just a new pair of trainers and maybe a running watch. For now my investments were limited to new padded Lycra shorts, a new cycling top (one with pockets in the back to carry things), and a helmet (compulsory, I'd never owned one before this), and gloves (for my Raynaud's, hands go so numb I can't feel the brakes or gears).

I had entered the middle distance, 50 miles, and it went well. Knowing full well this was a non-competitive bike ride, I still set off like an idiot, overtaking as many people as possible, not knowing about the cycling etiquette of warning others of potholes, drains and gravel (there appears to be a whole unwritten rule book on these topics, it wasn't in the race briefing), and probably ended up upsetting many people with my competitive streak. I worked out that despite having a pretty basic bike and weighing more than most cyclists, the strength in my legs made up for this and resulted in me being a fairly decent cyclist, especially on hills when apparently heavy people are not so go (gravity pulls us back down).

What I'm not so good at is map reading, I had no Garmin bike computer so hadn't uploaded a map and didn't bother taking a paper version of the route, so I had to rely on course markings and following other riders. I whizzed around the course until around mile 48, at this point the field had thinned out so I hadn't seen anyone for ages apart from what looked like some short course riders, so guessed I was doing well for time. I noticed one person up ahead who seemed to be going as a decent speed so decided to do one last push, overtake him and then cross the finish line with my arms held high in jubilation just as I'd seen on the Tour de France.

With my final surge I caught and overtook this guy, then got to a T-junction; problem was there were no signs to tell me left or right. I used some male intuition and though right would take me in the direction of the finish line, but the rider I overtook swept past me and took left, so I followed and chased after him. Eventually I pulled up alongside and spoke to him, I said something like "crikey, this course appears to be far longer than 50 miles", at which point he looked at me puzzled. He said "what do you mean", and then I looked at his bike and realised he had no bike number attached. The conversation could have come out of a comedy sketch, it turned out I'd chased after a social cyclist who was not taking part in the race at all, I had concentrated on the rider and not the course and was now lost.

I said an embarrassed farewell and set off in a slightly stressed state, I had no idea where I was but would not admit defeat, no need to phone Sally or the organisers. I was disappointed as had a feeling I would have crossed the finish line as one of the first riders, but to pick myself I kept reminding myself that it's not a race, there was no finishing times, no podium placing's, it was just for fun ! Eventually I found my way back, approaching the finishing line from a different direction confusing the marshals and other riders, deciding honesty was the best policy so owned up to my mistake at the check in desk at the end.

I collected my medal, bored Sally with my story while tucking into the free lunch provided at the end. Despite the ace bikes, and what appeared to be a far "posher" crowd (based on their accents and cars) than I had met a running races, the atmosphere at the end was fantastic, really friendly, which was nice as during the race it was not so sociable – maybe this was because I was concentrating on racing though.

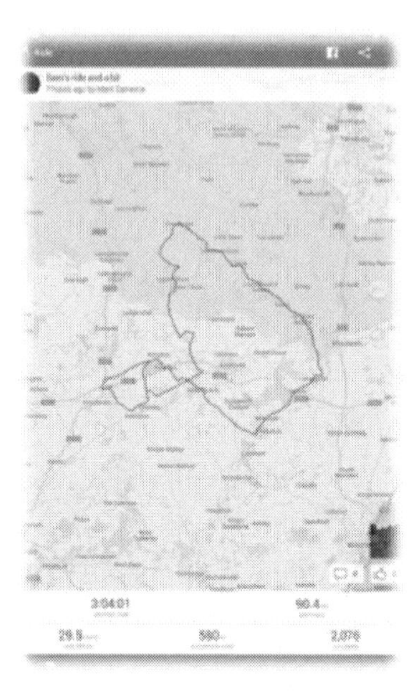


This is when I started to get more interested in cycling, what was originally a rehab activity and a backup plan was turning into an opportunity to do something new, not something I'd concentrate on so much yet since I knew I hadn't fully realised my running potential – the way I see things is if I have 100% of my focus and time available, I could either put 100% into one sport and be the best I can, or split the 100% between multiple sports and just be good at all of them. This applies to work as well as home/social life, I'm an all or nothing kind of person, I prefer one big project which makes a big impact, rather than many small ones where I seem to spend a lot of effort and time trying to prioritise, pleasing far too many people, and results are not as good as expected.

I would recommend cycling to anyone, it's not only a good way to exercise but it's also an inexpensive method of transport. I now notice those quiet cyclists who get on their bikes early in the morning and cycle to work, not for a medal or a finish time, but simply to get to work. In the past I barely noticed them, a little like runners – before I started running I didn't pay any attention to them, now I notice loads.

Learning point from this race, cross training is good for you, it works new muscles but also leads to new opportunities – if I hadn't had my injury I wouldn't have started cycling so much, any spare time would be spent overtraining on the running, and if I hadn't started cycling I would not have had the pleasure of completing my first bike race.

## Step counting – Trionium Munro (14/06)

**Midsummer Munro**

**'The hardest half'**

Box Hill Fort, at the TOP of Box Hill, Surrey, UK, KT20 7LB

8am Sunday 14 June 2015

NOTE NEW START TIME!

I was meant to be doing the Three Peaks Challenge at the time of this race but I decided to pull out at the last minute. I was a little disappointed with this, to go and climb the three highest peaks in Scotland, England and Wales in one day would have been great, but I knew my leg wasn't in a good shape, I didn't want to slow others down (although Carlos the organiser assured me speed wasn't important), and more importantly I didn't want to run the risk of my leg failing and then screwing things up for others. In a running race things are slightly different, if the leg gives way then the race continues, in this event I would cause problems for everyone else in our group which to me didn't seem fair. So having made the decision, I had to find an alternative (well I didn't HAVE to, but I wanted to), so I scoured the internet and found this event. It attracted my attention as I'd heard of Box Hill, but never been there (it's at the north point of the South Downs, about 19 miles south of London), plus the title "The Hardest Half" was tempting me.

Why was it being called the hardest? Well it turns out the clue is in the title, it's a Munro which is defined as

Munro

/mʌnˈrəu/

*noun*

any of the 277 mountains in Scotland that are at least 3,000 feet high (approximately 914 metres).

So it's a half marathon up a hill called box hill in Surrey, with an elevation gain of around 3,000 feet, quite a lot of gain per km run. Linking back to my thinking that everything must have a purpose, this was perfect preparation for the Sky race, this race being just under half the distance of the Sky race and also just under half the elevation.

My leg was slowly improving so I starting running a few more hills in preparation for this event. I love hills, I'm not that good at them (I'm happy to accept the reason I learnt from the cyclists, gravity acts hardest on heavier people), but I love the challenge of getting to the top, plus the views are always great from higher up. The good thing about going up hills is it slows me down, I can't run fast even if I wanted to so it's better for my leg, the problem is on the downhill where the pressure on my shin would be worse – I got around this by going down pretty slowly, sometimes the downhill pace being pretty much the same as the uphill pace.

To motivate myself further for hills I entered a climbing challenge on Strava, run 6,600 feet over 3 weeks. I found myself obsessed with this challenge, setting my alarm for 4am during the week and driving to Butser Hill to run before work. I ended up completing over 18,000 feet over those 3 weeks, mega kudos ☺ , which culminated in one final test run of 10 miles and 700 feet of gain up and down Butser Hill, just 3 days before the race (will never get the hang of these tapers). There was no major reaction after than run so I knew I was good to go.

The race location was around 100k away, the start time 8am, but despite the distance and start time we decided to drive up on the day, we were sure the roads would be quiet which they were. The event was really well organised at the start, free coffee to get me warmed up, and a singing of the national anthem at the start to warm us up even further. I have no idea why the anthem was sung, looking a previous race reports it looks like a tradition of the organisers, no bad thing to be patriotic so good for them.

About 200 people entered, we finished our singing and the horn went, we were off

.........and then we stopped. The course start line was new versus previous years, we ran straight into a bottleneck, a single file trail, so all apart from the front runners backed up and had to all shuffle

forward. Once we got past this area the path opened up, we were at the top of Box Hill with magnificent views ahead of us and a guy in a kilt playing bagpipes

We raced down the hill, and then at the bottom turned round and trudged back up it. This set the scene for the rest of the race, basically up and down Box Hill in as many different routes as possible.

The second route down was where the steps thing comes in, it was an old set of steps, some uneven, some very steep, where again most people went single file downwards.

At the bottom we crossed a river via a bridge, and then turned around and crossed the river via some stepping stones. For most this was fine, for me with a bad leg (sorry to keep going on about it), stepping one foot at a time was not great, I had been practicing standing one footed on my bad leg, but wet steps with tired legs, plus the pressure of others queued behind was not great – as you can see here

The race continued in a familiar routine, up the hill, down the hill, sometimes more steps, sometimes grassy slopes, even one particularly steep mud/wood section which some poor woman end up falling at and needed medical help.

I carried a hand held water bottle, the kind that has a built in handle, which seemed to work ok. My grip was not so good due to the Raynaud's so I was constantly switching it between hands, giving one a rest and to get feeling back in it while using the other. I had a pre-workout mixture in this bottle and used the many aid stations to swig water and grab jelly sweets.

Because of the hills the pace wasn't so fast, I managed to really enjoy myself at a sensible pace without having many people overtake me; I even managed short conversations with other runners as we went.

I ended up crossing the line in 2 hr 22 minutes, 71st out of 189 starters, a slow time versus my previous half marathon but based on the Three Forts performance it was a definite improvement.

We got given carrots at the end (no idea why), medals, a finishers T-Shirt which had all the runners names printed on the back, plus a picnic to tuck into which included sandwiches, savouries, and cake. I'm going to award this race the title of "Best surprise of the year", this was a last minute decision to enter the race as a substitute for not doing the 3 Peaks, but it turned out to be a really great day; it was well organised, had a great atmosphere, brilliant location, and I had a lot of fun. Sally also enjoyed herself walking up and down some of the steps while she waited for me; this was a wise move for her as there was less need for me to bore her with my story afterwards.

What were my learning points from this race? Firstly, out of adversity comes opportunities, I would never have done this if I hadn't pulled out of the Three Peaks. Secondly, fuel choice was great, no need to stress over taking too much on such a race, research fuel points and then work backwards from there – too often last year I would plan what to take and then work forwards, by this I mean I'd pack my fuel, start the run, and then find loads of food and drink along the way. It's like process mapping at work, work backwards through the process. Problem is with this last point is I often forget the basics like this, I would no doubt still make the same mistakes again in the future but then no one is perfect, it's just about making the same mistakes less often.

After this I had just 7 weeks until the Sky race, I was cutting things a little fine to prepare but the dream was becoming more and more possible in my mind now.

## Holiday – Stop being so selfish

Immediately after the Munro race Sally and I went on holiday. We always try to go on holiday in June and October, it's when each of us age another year (i.e. our birthdays). This year we decided to stay local, so went to Tenerife. I really should have seen this as a rest week, time to get some warm weather on my rapidly healing leg, but my paranoia with my weight and body fat (hang up from body building days, could almost call it an eating disorder), meant there was no way I could do an all-inclusive holiday, eat and drink whilst not exercising, and enjoy myself.

Our hotel was lovely, it was an eco-resort, in the South of the island, right next to a canyon with nature trails to walk (or run). Either side of the rest there were dormant volcanoes, one about 5 miles away, the other 3 miles away. Needless to say I ran to both of these, and then also up them, which normally would be quite a short run however in the heat and with the alcohol and food sloshing around inside me, this felt much harder than usual.

I struggled on, completing several 10 mile runs, but wasn't really enjoying it. I was hot, I was struggling, I was tired and not relaxing, plus I was spending time away from Sally on what was meant to be her birthday holiday. We were also celebrating 20 years together and our 11th wedding anniversary, I should have been visiting these wonderful places I was running to with her – coming back with photos and stories was really selfish of me. It was at this point I re-evaluated things, deciding to go totally against my plans and to cut back training, do shorter runs, and focus more on the original purpose of running for me – to enjoy myself regardless of the race time.

I found the Asics app on my tablet and set up a marathon training plan which involved shorter runs. My ultra's were only 50k's, just 5 miles longer than a marathon, so if I wasn't so bothered with the finish time then this would be fine. The plan also had the bonus of 3 mile runs on most Saturdays; this meant I could do Parkrun's as part of this plan. Since the Peak Sky race was literally weeks away, and the plan produced by the app was a full 16 week plan, I decided to just follow the final 7 weeks of the plan, a bonus was it had a 3 week taper period so not many more long runs to do, I felt immediately better.

The rest of my holiday was so much better after this, we had a great time, and I chilled out and slept loads by the pool. We went on some long walks together, me dragging Sally (who has a fear of heights) up some volcanoes (including a special happy birthday / wedding anniversary hike up Mount Guaza).

Birthday girl thinking how the hell will I get down?

I don't tell her often enough that I love her – love her company, love her kindness, love her cakes

## Another sportive, further and higher this time – Portsmouth Sportive (28/06)

So we got back from holiday on Saturday, 27th June, and I'd entered this bike race as a way to get me back into a long distance mind-set in an easy way. This was longer and higher than Sam's ride, 90km and around 1,000 metres in total, but a long distance on a bike feels so much easier than one on my feet, hence the decision to do this so soon after my holiday.

This was another sportive, not an official bike race, but one I still wanted to push myself on. It was called the Portsmouth Sportive, the only thing "Portsmouth" about it was the start line, thankfully the course was not 90km cycling around the flat urban rounds of Portsea island (I think we would have had to do at least 3 laps of the entire city to even make 90km), instead the route took us immediately out of Portsmouth and into the peace and tranquillity of the South Downs. We didn't see Portsmouth again until the end of the race.

I had taken the opportunity while on holiday to order myself a new Garmin bike computer, nothing flashy, just a 500 model, but there was no point spending more, it did all I needed it to do and to have expensive kit on a cheap bike would be a dumb thing to do. I also went and bought my first pair of clip on pedals which I fitted Saturday evening, I'd heard it made your cycling more efficient, especially uphill, so I decided to take the risk of trying them. I'm useless at anything related to DIY so while switching pedals I stripped the thread on my old ones, I therefore had no choice but to ride with the new pedals – to ease my worry I decided to not test them until the race, if I had tested them and decided I didn't like them I had no choice anyway, I had no old pedals left. Sally was slightly worried by this last point, especially since I have a habit of falling over when running and off on bikes, but I told her I would be fine and would ride to the start line to test them, this possibly worried her even more.

A short mention of the process to buy these pedals and how it links back to my job of challenging stupid processes, little things like this wind me up so much. I bought them from Halfords after seeing them online where they were advertised as reduced from £30 to £17. I went into the local branch to buy them and luckily they had them in stock, but at the full price of £30. I questioned the price but was told that the reduced price was an online special, not available in store. My brain went to work quickly, how could I get around this – clichés like "this outside the box" and "challenge the process" sprung to mind, just as they do every day. I stepped out of the store, ordered the pedals online, selected "collect at local store", got an order confirmation, then went back into the store with my order number, paid for and picked up the pedals at the reduced price. How stupid are some shops? The store assistant knew what I'd done since he was the one who told me originally they couldn't price match, he told me their online shop competes with the high street shop. If I were a consultant looking at this I would have told them they would have been far better off having the same price and using the time I was in the store to upsell goods such as the range of cycling tops I was eyeing up – too bad, no time to upsell this time, their own fault.

I had an easy start to the race day; woke up, grabbed some porridge and an espresso, and then cycled off to the start line which was maybe 30 minutes cycle ride away. I hadn't trained for this event, I don't feel the need to train so hard for such events, cycling feels so much easier than running – you learn it at a young age, you grow stronger with age so you should automatically get better, if you're training to compete then it's going to be different but to take part in a sportive (which is meant to be for fun) then I think it should be that simple. The only thing I ever stress over with cycling is getting a puncture because I have absolutely no idea how to change an inner tube on a bike, because of this I don't bother to carry anything with me to do such repairs, if I get a puncture then I would probably simply phone Sally and ask her to come pick me up and then have to worry about how the hell she will find me. I guess this last point reflected my whole attitude towards competing in running and cycling at this time, especially cycling, where just taking part is enough for me to have a good time.

I turned up at the start in one piece, learning very quickly that when you have your feet locked into the pedals it's a good plan to approach red traffic lights really, really, slowly, and try to reach them just as they are changing colour, and worst case scenario look out for the nearest post to lean against rather than try unclipping in front of bemused drivers.

When I arrived I got talking to a few people at the start line, as had happened at Sam's ride I found myself admiring their really cool bikes and comparing to my bike which was rapidly increasing in value due to new pedals, a tri-bar I'd got off e-bay (really useful to have these when you suffer from numb fingers a lot), my bike computer, and all the bike clothing I'd bought.

We were due to go off in small waves about 2 minutes apart, I was planning to go as early as possible as I wanted to get home in time for lunch, when one of the cyclists behind me said "you're not going to ride on that are you?" I wasn't sure how to react, conscious of my bike I thought he was one of these bike snobs and was referring to the make/model/frame material, but I stayed calm and asked "what do you mean?" He pointed to my rear tyre, which I had presumed was just muddy, however on closer inspection it turned out the mud was in fact the webbing showing through the tyre rubber, my tyre was pretty much bald – front and back! I tried to stay calm, inside I was worrying as I knew this would only enhance the chance of a puncture, and just told him "I didn't have time to change them, will do so at the end".

We set off in a group of around 20, straight out of Portsmouth, up a hill, I was at the back trying to keep up, but somehow never letting the others lose me – I think this was in fear of me being dropped by the group and then struggling to find the route on my own (bike computer did basic maps, but I hadn't had time to work out how to download the map, I was just using it for distance, speed and elevation). The course was local, but as with running it took me through areas I knew but routes I had no idea of.

As we moved on through the course I was getting more and more confident with my clip in pedals, because we were out in the country we didn't have many problems with road junctions or traffic, I hadn't fallen off once and I don't remember ever needing to stop. I used a strategy of whizzing past fuel stations so that I did not have to worry about trying to unclip in front of people.

The fuel stop plan worked well, I overtook loads by skipping these stations, I think my slow pace at the start was also paying off (negative splits work on a bike just as well as on your feet), and my strong legs which I'd used so often as an excuse for slow running and major cramps, were really helping on hills (the theory of heavy cyclists struggling uphill is probably true, but strong legs help reduce the effect).

All the time I was wary of my bald tyres, I kept asking myself "why do they have so much gravel on country lanes", but there was nothing much I could do about this, I just tried not to skid, for once also avoiding potholes and drains, and prayed they held out (which they did).

I feel quite alone while cycling, I am pretty quick on a bike but the other quick cyclists are often what I'd call "pack riders" who cycle in groups, often being a pain by cycling abreast of each other and holding up other traffic which gives cyclists a bad name. The more sociable cyclists seem to be midpoint or even further back, but I'm too impatient to cycle with them, hence just going off on my own. I did a lot of thinking on the bike while I was alone, it was a chance to enjoy myself but instead I kept pondering about things like "why on earth am I doing this", I did this last year while running (what makes me happy), I don't know the answer to this and many other questions I ask myself, I just end up making myself aware of the question, and then continue to look for an answer.

At 40 miles I found myself starting to recognise where I was, had not seen another cyclist (at least any in the event) for some time, but because I knew the route home I gained in confidence, picked up speed, and headed back to the finish line. The Garmin was doing its job, I was doing the maths in my head, average speed (not pace, I'm cycling not running), distance to travel, estimated finish time, etc., and motivating myself to go harder and faster. Because I knew the route from here I also knew what to expect in terms of hills, just 2 biggies to go, and I was also sure that if the dreaded puncture occurred I'd be able to guide Sally to where I was.

I got to the first of these two hills and at last encountered another cyclists crawling up the hill. I caught and overtook him, saying hello as I went past but then on the downhill he caught me again (weird as I thought heavy people were faster downhill, I was definitely heavier). I remembered the mistake from Sam's ride, I didn't want to get side-tracked by someone not on the same event, so I checked with him that he was doing the Sportive, which he was. I have no idea where he'd come from, how he'd got in front of me, and I didn't catch his name (a South African guy is all I remember), but he was a really nice guy - my definition of nice here is that he didn't shoot off and leave me.

We cycled all the way back to the finish line, chatting away, when we got to the finish line and I did a sneaky dip ahead of him at the end, finishing my longest ever ride of 92km and over 1,000 metres of elevation gain, in 3 hours 17 minutes, and still feeling pretty fresh – I'd felt far worse after many half marathons. This finish line was a huge anti-climax, when we left there were quite a few people and music playing, when we arrived back there was no music and hardly anyone around. The organisers told us we were the first to cross the line and that we'd finished sooner than they'd expected so hadn't set up yet, I'm not so sure of this, it was their first year of the event so will give them the benefit of the doubt. While talking they noticed by tyres asking "how did you manage that ride on those tyres?" I told them I'd taken it easy (I kind of had done), but then used the bike mechanics from a local shop to supply and fit me with new tyres front and back – my cheap bike was becoming an even more expensive bike, £60 for 2 tyres!

So that was it, my second sportive completed. I ended up finishing 3rd overall, missing second by 30 seconds. I did enjoy the event; I think part of the enjoyment was caused out of guilt since it meant I'd burnt off a huge amount of the calories I'd consumed while on holiday. I won't deny it was also good to place 3rd; my competitive streak was still alive somewhere inside me. Since the bodybuilding I hadn't got a podium place at anything sport related so was also desperate for some kind of placing – deep down, despite being intent on enjoying races, nothing beats the feeling of success.

Search results (Showing 1-10 of 58)

| No. | Name | Chip Time ▼ | Gender | Cat |
| --- | --- | --- | --- | --- |
| 1484 | [illegible] | 2:54:36 | Male | Medium |
| 1085 | [illegible] | 3:16:31 | Male | Medium |
| 1344 | [illegible] | 3:17:49 | Male | Medium |

What would I do differently in future, absolutely nothing, it was such a relaxed ride, I rode further and higher than ever before, the tyres held out and I got a podium. A downside of coming straight from a holiday to this event was there was no cake at the end for me, disappointing but probably just as well as I'd eaten so much on holiday.

## Chapter 7: The foot race – Summer Plod (05/07)

The Portsmouth Sportive was the start of what was meant to be a gradual taper into the highlight of my year, the Peak District Sky race (sorry to keep mentioning that name but it really was a huge deal for me), however it seemed to be turning out to be a really busy period of running in races.

Another friend of mine, Kiernan Easton, had mentioned a local 21 mile, 720 metre elevation gain, trail race called the Summer Plod. It was only up the road from me, again near the South Downs, I saw this as another gradual step towards the distance and elevation of the Peak race so I entered it.

The day before the race I also decided to enter my first Parkrun of the year, actually it was only my second ever Parkrun, stupid me entered a fast course along Southsea seafront (flat, out and back), rather than one of the other local ones (we have lots nearby) which were included trails and hills. I will do a section on Parkrun's later in this book so will just say that on this occasion I turned up, naïve as hadn't done any 5k's this year, and just blasted out and back, classic positive split strategy, had a good time but possibly not the wisest thing to do before the Plod the next day.

For the plod I decided to wear a new pair of trail trainers, I know it's a stupid move which I'd done before and regretted, but I really couldn't decide on what to wear. I had loads of trainers at home; my Kalenji trail shoes had the deepest lugs so as it was trail which I'd been told got quite muddy I decided to use these instead of road running or hybrid shoes. I also decided to trial my Innov8 ultra vest which I'd bought, a little over the top for 21 miles but felt I was being sensible testing it in advance of bigger races.

As usual I was seeing this as a training run at an organised race, a chance to meet with friends, so hadn't worried about a taper (hence the parkrun) or diet leading up to this, perhaps I getting complacent at races by this point? We set off from a local Scout hut in Clanfield, I quickly realised that the warning of mud was maybe a little exaggerated, we hadn't had a warm summer but it had been dry, the ground was rock hard. To make matters worse, a lot of the course was on tarmac, even harder, and the new shoes were not working, in fact they were really uncomfortable. I was still carrying my injured right leg, landing much heavier on my good leg to compensate, and this heavy landing was causing me lots of pain in my good foot.

The race went okay overall, I would be lying if I said I loved it, some highlights were

- Catching up with Kiernan at the start, despite wanting it to be a social race I left him quite early when I got frustrated being held up by others on a hill
- Fuel choice was spot on; the ultra-vest did its job really well, a wise investment but not fool proof, as the next race would prove. I drank plenty as I went around and ate sensibly
- There was a chalk lane which seemed to go uphill for ages, it was only 2km long but it was at mile 15. The track was really rutted, really hard ground, not great in the heavy lugged trainer, this is me towards the end of this stage, struggling! I think this is where I damaged my feet most

- The pain in my feet from the trainers was agonising, especially across the final 4 miles, starting with the chalk lane and then roads all the way back, I was limping really bad by the end

I eventually crossed the line in 3 hrs 25 minutes, placed 14$^{th}$ out of 71, a pace of about 6 min per km. I'd been going really well until the feet started hurting at 18km, then I slowed down until 28km, finally speeding up towards the finish line so as not to embarrass myself at the finish line.

Sally met me at the end by which point I could hardly walk; she helped me limp to the race headquarters. My bad leg had held out fine, but my good leg now had a really bad foot.

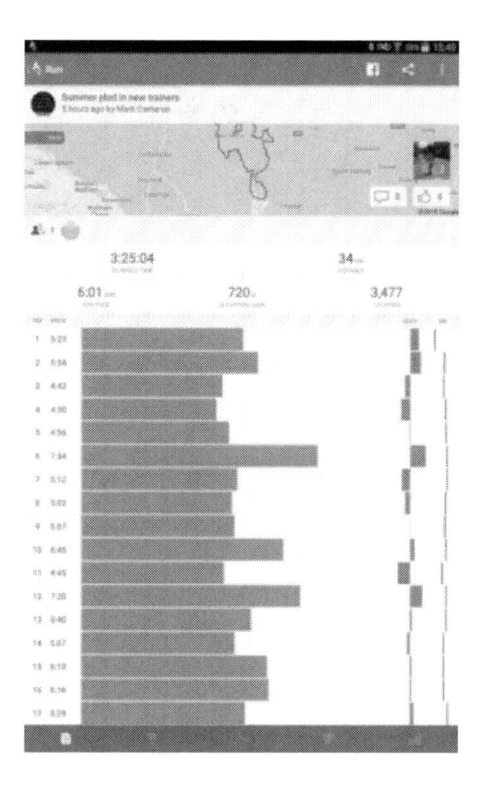


I sat down in the Scout hut, drinking hot chocolate and eating cake and fruit, I was putting off taking my shoes off as I really didn't want to see the mess I knew I'd find.

We hobbled back to the car where I then removed my shoe. What a mess, huge blisters on the sore foot, and worse still, 2 toenails hanging off on the good leg, this was a real worry with longer races coming up soon.

I put on a brave face, not a lot I could do about this really, popped the blisters, removed the toe nails, soaked my feet in Epsom salts, and learnt for next time.  I don't think new shoes were the problem, they fitted fine, I think it was the shoe choice versus the race surface.  The shoes could have been well worn, I probably still would have chosen them for the day, but the surface was way too hard, it reminded me of when I was younger and would wear football boots on tarmac after a game, you could feel the studs through the sole of the shoes every step you took, so uncomfortable.

As was traditional for races, I had even more cake when I got home, Sally had made a cobbler using allotment grown rhubarb. Many people I know don't like rhubarb, even those who grow it in allotments seem to try giving it away, yet go into a shop and it's expensive, I love the stuff.

My learnings from this race would be to stop being so casual about races, I need to plan better in future, to learn from previous experience (I get older, but maybe not always wiser), to treat every race like a race, even if you are not racing it (does that make sense?). I would recommend the event to anyone who wants to do something in-between a half and a full marathon, it was very well organised, good fuel stations, lots of marshals on course, and the scenery was fabulous – not sure if I'd be saying the same if it had been muddy though ☺

I put this quote at the end of this chapter as I think it sums up how I felt at this point, things were getting tougher in my mind and my body, but I kept looking at pictures of the Peak District to remind myself where I was heading, it really helped motivate me and keep me going as my feet were (and still are now) in a right mess.

## Drink you idiot – Chiltern Ultra (11/07)

On my warm up journey to the Peak Sky race, I entered the Meon race from the previous chapter. That race was Kiernan's warm up to this race, the Chiltern Ultra. I'm far too easily led into entering races, I noticed he'd entered this Ultra so decided to do the same – I looked at it as the final warm up to my "A" race for the year. Race distance was 50km, just over 1,000 metres of ascent, so same horizontal distance to Peak race, but about half the vertical distance, I figured it would be a good indication of how I'd get on in the Peak District, in hindsight I may have been pushing my luck a little here as it was just 6 days between the Meon race and this one, then 3 more weeks until the Sky race.

This race was also just around the corner from where Jacob lived so I contacted him and encouraged him to also take part, it was slightly more expensive than other races but he had far less travel to get there and no hotel to worry about, so overall cost was going to be cheaper than it first appeared (links back to my day job, think of the overall process, not just the part you are interested in). Jacob signed up, as expected he studied the race really thoroughly, checking the elevation and previous results, planning out his race strategy and hoped to finish in sub 4.5 hours, this was definitely possible based on his weekly 50k training runs, but I did mention to him that a race on an unfamiliar course would test him more than maybe he expected. Look at me, giving out advice when I don't even listen to myself, god I hate people like that!

Being very risk averse (not helped by working in insurance), I always worry far too much about my old car breaking down on the way to races, so I booked into a hotel near to the race venue the night before. We travelled up after work Friday, the hotel was actually a pub with rooms about a 15 minute drive from the start line, it was cheap and basic, but did the job. I took my usual over-sized picnic with me for the night before, far too much food. Somehow I managed most of it, plus a cheeky small bottle of wine, which Sally and I enjoyed the night before the race while watching junk TV on the smallest hotel TV I'd ever seen.

The race was run by a well-known company called X-NRG (Extreme Energy), and was really well organised as you'd expect from such a company. This was actually a fairly small event for them as they are better known for multi-day events such as the Around the Isle of Wight, Pony Express, and Pilgrim Challenge races.

We drove through a housing estate to get to the start line, I began worrying about the terrain being similar to the Meon race as I saw all the tarmac around me, the detail on the website said it was a trail race, I knew I couldn't afford to make the same mistake as in the Meon race as this was a longer race plus my feet were in pieces from the last race. I actually planned a bit better at this race, covering a few bases on this occasion by taking 2 different pairs of trainers so I could decide on which to wear on the day. I was not going to try full trail trainers as last time, I learnt my lesson the hard way, so had a pair of Asics hybrid trail/road trainers, and also my very well worn pair of Asics road shoes. Initially I went for the hybrids, but when I pulled them on I had a change of mind – they felt a little tight with the thick socks I had decided to use, so I had no choice and went for the road shoes. As part of my planning I had what I thought was the great idea to download the race course GPX file onto my Garmin bike computer and use this as a backup in case I got lost, there was no need to buy yet another item of tech (GPS tracker/watch with map function) as I had originally thought of doing. This bike computer handily clipped onto one of the gel loops on the shoulder strap of my ultra-vest, such a wise decision, I was learning.

I warmed up a little (well jumped up and down on the spot), ate even more food, and strapped on my Ultra race vest. I had filled up the 2 half litre bottles on the shoulder straps with carb drinks, decided not to use the hydration bladder as there were plenty of fuel stops along the way, and filled up some of the remaining compartments with fuel such as more carb powder and gels.

The race had 2 start times for the Ultra, one for sub 6 hour runners and the other an hour earlier for all others. I put myself into the 6+ hours group, I aimed for 5 to 6 hours but didn't want to put pressure on myself to run too hard as I had my big race 3 weeks later, plus Jacob was planning on finishing faster than me so I thought getting an hour head start would mean he wouldn't have to wait too long after finishing for me.

They also had options for walkers to do the course (even earlier start) plus a "half-ultra" option of 25km. Another person I knew from social media, Sharla McTavish, was running this option so I made contact with her before the race and arranged to meet up to say hello to each other. It was great to meet her at the start line; she was starting at the same time as me but would definitely finish well before me so I didn't see her after the race. It was also good timing as Jacob turned up at the same time, we managed a group photograph before Sharla and I headed off for the start line, Jacob went to get ready for his start an hour later. I also hooked up with Kiernan at this point, I seem to remember this being his first Ultra, or maybe he'd had a DNF in the past, not sure but good to see him there. He had driven up on the day with his friend Paul Spooner; this was to be Pauls 100th race of marathon distance or further, awesome achievement.

The weather was perfect for me, sunny and warm, in hindsight maybe not perfect for running, but I'm definitely a warm weather runner (it helps with the Raynaud's problem although I still get cold and numb hands). I set off with Kiernan, middle of the pack, then similar to the Meon race within a few hundred metres the run slowed to a hike, partially caused by a small hill, partially caused by the path becoming very narrow and a huge bottleneck building up. I hate it when this happens, the Trionium Munro was pretty bad but only lasted a short distance, and this was seemed to go on forever as it was uphill. My impatience was being tested here so I apologised to Kiernan and set off to try weaving my way through the line of people ahead.

The race was thankfully pretty much 100% trail, up and down hills, through fields, one slightly boggy section as we came to the end. I initially doubted my shoe choice, running up and down hill was not so easy in the road shoes (as I said, they were pretty worn out, if they were tyres they'd be called slicks), but this actually worked in my favour a little as it made me slow down quite a lot on the hills and preserve any unnecessary stress on my leg which was still causing me problems.

I reached the halfway point fairly easily, about 2.5 hours, so well on track for the 5(ish) hour finish time. The race was well signposted up to this point, good fuel stops which I briefly stopped at, but then at mile 18 things started to go wrong.

First problem was my leg starting to get sore, not so surprising as I hadn't run this distance that often, plus I was running awkward due to not only the sore right leg but also the damage on my left foot from the previous race. On top of this, I got slightly lost on my own in a field, I couldn't see any tape directing me out of the field and there were a herd of cows looking at me threateningly. I tried to use the provided paper map but this had unfortunately disintegrated in the sweat in my shorts, then tried the Garmin bike computer to find my route but at this point was starting to panic a little, I was not thinking clearly, so hung around hoping for some other runners to turn up which thankfully they did.

The great thing about ultra's is that although we all want to do the best we can, we also have time to help and encourage each other. I'd say they are less about racing and more about experiences. We found the route out of the field, headed along a road, and then met up with yet more runners looking for route markings. I used my GPS map on the bike computer to point the direction we should be heading, and as we set off we started finding race marker tape hidden in bushes. There are some totally idiots in this world who have such sad lives and wish to try making others have lives as miserable as theirs. In running these are often the people who decide its great fun to sabotage races by moving signs and tearing down markers, and in this race we were facing similar problems. We met up with two kids who were obviously the guilty parties, a couple of runners shouted at them as they saw them tearing down the markers we had put back up, but the kids simply ignored us and continued. We told marshals at the next checkpoint and carried on, we found out later it wasn't just kids doing this, there was some old lady (use that term loosely) who was also doing similar as she was against a race taking part through what I presume she thought was "her land" (it was actually public footpaths).

So I was now running with others, but still struggling really bad. Determined to learn from previous experiences I decided to start run/walking, and then it became more of a walk/walk/walk/run (i.e. much less running). This was me trying to be sensible, the race was about me gaining experience, I had plenty of time to finish in around 6 hours, I was actually quite proud of myself for doing this but then also slightly disappointed that I was still going and hadn't just decided to stop and save my leg. The reason for me taking this option was I truly believed it was my head and lack of conditioning telling me to stop, my leg was hurting but I wasn't limping or walking awkward, if anything just the thought of not finishing in 5 hours was demotivating me a little, so I dug in and kept going.

That second half of the race seemed to take forever, I had ticked over at around 6 min per km in the first half and slowed to around 8 ½ min per km in the second half. I don't remember too much about that second half apart from the route markers, my head was a blur and I'd realise why later on. I did run with a few different runners along the way, one of them was James Heggie who I met at the finish line and then again at a future race in the year. He kept me going, happy to run/walk with me, but then as we neared the end and headed down a rather steep hill, I urged him to run on as there was no way I was going to risk a DNF by running downhill so close to the finish line. I also remember not seeing Jacob overtake me along the way, it was my expectation he would have come past with around 6 to 8 miles to go (my original plan to finish at around the same time of the day as him was based on a 5 hr finish time, I was now on track for around 6 hours). He did eventually catch and pass me on this final downhill section, probably just a mile or two from the finish line, so his original plan of finishing sub 4 ½ hours had obviously also not worked out for him.

I crossed the line in 6 hr 3 minutes, feeling pretty good at the end, my feet were hurting far less than at the end of 21 miles on the Meon race and wasn't suffering from cramps as bad as usual, I did have what felt like waterlogged ears but ignored this thinking it was just sweat or too much drink wishing around inside me. I collected my medal and went into the school hall where Jacob and Vicky were waiting, along with loads of cakes and drinks.

Unheard of for me, I had no appetite at all for cake, I felt sick if anything, very weird feeling as I love cake and usually crave food after running, but I drank a few cups of tea and sat down for an hour or so chatting away. After chatting away we decided to head back home so headed up some steps out of the hall.

That was the last thing I remembered for a while, this is the next thing I remembered....

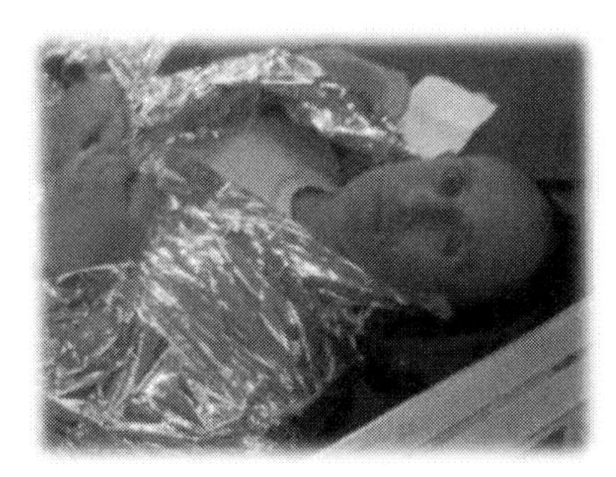

I have been called irresponsible for posting this picture on social media by some, I look terrible and felt pretty bad, but I think awareness of problems and key learning points (whether for me or for others) can only be listened to when the truth is shown. We see pictures of people crossing the finish line, often looking so fresh, arms in the air and sprinting the last few yards, and this is the view I had of running. Because of this I pushed myself harder and harder, thinking it was easy, as I said in a previous chapter I was getting complacent thinking it's just 52,000 steps to complete a marathon, and totally ignored the dangers such as damaged feet, serious injuries, or as I had found out in this race, the important of nutrition.

On this occasion I had passed out while walking up the steps out of the building. I simply blacked out, fell backwards, hit my head, and was awoken by the sound of Sally, medics, and others around me asking if I was ok. It felt like I'd just had a seriously deep sleep and was being woken up, I had hit my head hard but no bruising, bumps, or blood. As I said at the start of this chapter (sorry it's a long chapter), the race was organised by X-NRG, a really professional outfit who had medics onsite who immediately took great care of me. My heart beat and blood pressure were really low; these measurements wouldn't go back up even after an hour waiting and some sweet cups of tea. Medics asked me if I'd remembered to drink during the race and I replied I had drunk so much I had stopped as could feel "swishing" in my stomach and in-between my ears. It turned out I was severely dehydrated, the water in my ears was a warning sign which I'd not been aware of at the time, as was me not thinking clearly while I was running (the lost in a field while trying to work GPS moment and not remembering too much about second half of the race were key warning signs), these were things I had never really experienced in the past, they are not mentioned so much in race reports that I had read or in race day strategy articles I had read, so I'd learnt the hard way.

After a couple of hours the vital signs started to recover, I felt terrible for Jacob and Vicky as I'd achieved my goal of not letting them wait too long for me to finish the race but now here they were, sitting with me waiting for me to recover. Once I'd started to feel better I encouraged them to head home, Sally would take good care of me, and the medics were happy for me to go home – so long as Sally drove me. I think her vital signs were going to go through the roof at this point, she doesn't like driving in strange locations plus I had no map or sat-nav for her to follow, just my own directions that were in my head. The thought of her driving along the M25 worried me a little; I think this may have helped raise my heart beat and blood pressure even faster.

Anyway, we got home fine, I felt good when we got in, managed a beer and Chinese takeaway so couldn't have been that bad. I unpacked my race kit and my ultra-vest was like an Aladdin's cave of goodies, I reckon I ended up finishing with more than I started with. Thinking a little clearer now and remembering what the medics said ("have you drunk much while running?"), I realised I had drunk the contents of my two water bottles, and refilled them, but never actually drank from them again. Apart from sips of water at the fuel stations, I had only drunk 1 litre of fluid, all carb mixture drinks, and eaten very little. As I said, it was a warm sunny days, I had skipped through the first 15 miles relatively easy, but then as the dehydration kicked in I started to slow down not only my running but also my entire body (including my thick head). As that shut down, things just got worse and worse, it was surprising I'd actually managed to finish the race. I took this very seriously, I'm not dismissing it as just something that happened, I actually went to the local doctors twice in the next month for further check-ups to make sure there was nothing long term to worry about. I was in perfect working order thank god, but this was a huge warning for me.

On a brighter note, that was it; my 3rd Ultra was now completed, despite the problems I think this was my best race up to this point. I use the term "best" in maybe a different context to how I would have done before the race, my day job is about spotting things which aren't working and looking for improvement options. For me, a perfect race, finished in a record time, is not a great learning opportunity, I wouldn't learn as much in it as from a race where I may struggle. In this race I entered it in pretty good shape physically (all things considered) and my kit choice was improving, so I was getting better at these parts, but had totally ignored to nutrition side of things. This is surprising as when bodybuilding I knew winning was 75% nutrition, maybe 15% training, and 10% genetics. In hindsight, alcohol the night before a race on a warm day is not the best idea ever (especially when inexperienced at such distances), even sticking to carb drinks is stupid; water mixed with electrolytes is also required. I learnt about the early warning signs of water in the ears, about losing your mind and not thinking rationally. Best of all, I was still fit and healthy, my leg actually felt stronger after this race, and I'd learnt all this before the Peak Sky race – if the same had happened there I don't know what I'd have done.

Final paragraph, what happened to Jacob in this race, why had he not overtaken me earlier? Turns out we both learnt something from this race. He had set off in the elite group like a greyhound, leading from the start, but took a wrong turn. He ran for an extra 5 miles before re-joining the course, but by the time he was back on course the sweeper had past him and started taking down the route markers (cleaning up the course, not to sabotage the course). Huge kudos to Jacob, he told me he became angry and disappointed at this, initially not understanding why the course markings had been taken down, but he also dug in, caught up with others and raced around the course finishing in around 5 hours. I know he was disappointed with the time, but I was chuffed he finished the race. He is naturally an amazing runner, he plans food and pacing miles better than me, but even the best runners can find opportunities to learn and I know he learnt from this. I'm pleased to also report Sharla and Kiernan also finished their races in good times and in one piece, Kiernan suffered a little with sickness along the way but finished well and I met with him at the end, Sharla finished way earlier than me and was well on the way home by the time I finished – hopefully we will meet up again in a future race. Paul also got his 100th marathon completed, nice one Paul.

Jacob looking fresh despite the extra 5 miles

Me looking fresh, definitely early on in the race

My medal, T-shirt, and unique finishing prizes of sick bowl and foil blanket

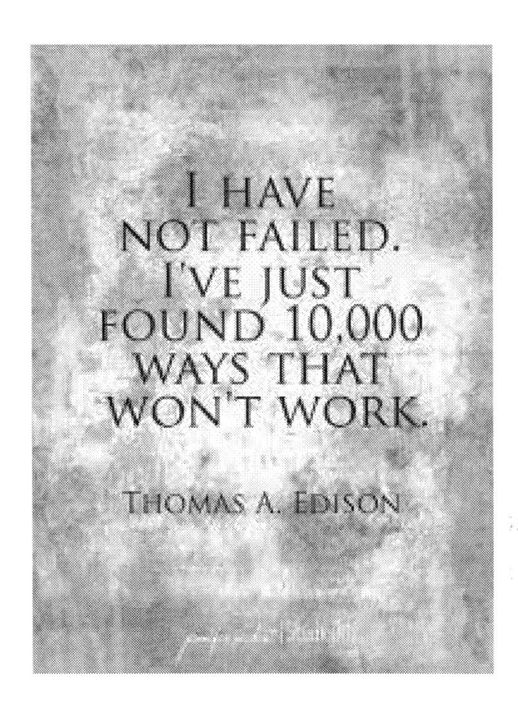


This says it all really, they say you need to repeat something 10,000 times before you perfect something, I'm never going to be a perfect runner, I'm going to run out of years, but I will improve every time – onto my next race, the Peak Sky race.

## The highlight of my running career so far – Peak Sky race (02/08)

Can't believe I made it to this chapter, the highlight of my year, something I entered while injured and without really thinking things through. I entered only having completed one flat ultra-marathon; I had no idea where the Peak District was, and couldn't walk, but was totally seduced by the website photos and the video's I'd seen of other Sky races. I never imagined I could enter such a race but then that's the great thing about running, it's a tough sport but not an elite sport, most races are open to pro's and novice's, it's a truly inclusive sport with very little snobbery, even at the start the best runners are happy to line up with novices like me which I find so inspiring.

The Peak District Sky race is organised by three great guys, Forest Bethell, Billy Craig, and Richard Weremiuk, all are experienced ultra-runners who are obviously hugely passionate about their sport and also this area of the country. The effort to stage such a race cannot be underestimated, despite running projects for a multi-national company I wouldn't know where to start on such an event, and guys like this (and many others who arrange similar races) do this not for the money (I'm pretty sure there's minimal if any cost/benefit), but because they love running.

The race was in its second year, starting in Buxton in the Peak District which I'm told is not in the North of England but in fact in the Midlands, it's North of London, so it's North to me. Buxton is a beautiful place, I imagined it as a small village with a babbling brook running through it, stupid me did this because I pictured the famous Buxton mineral water and nothing else. It is in fact a spa town, not the kind of town I know from down South with congestion and over-population, but a town with quiet roads, a wonderful park with an opera house overlooking it, and a decent array of shops including loads and loads of tea rooms. I honestly had never been somewhere like this in the UK before.

I had 3 weeks in between the Chiltern and Peak races, I decided to cut back on my running in this period, have a long taper, and invest the time that I wasn't running into reading up a lot of nutrition. I read the internet, I read books, I read my old race reports, and carefully wrote down a plan to ensure I learnt from the last episode. I also listened to Jacob and the in depth pace planning he did, the advice he gave me that I had wrongly laughed at previously.

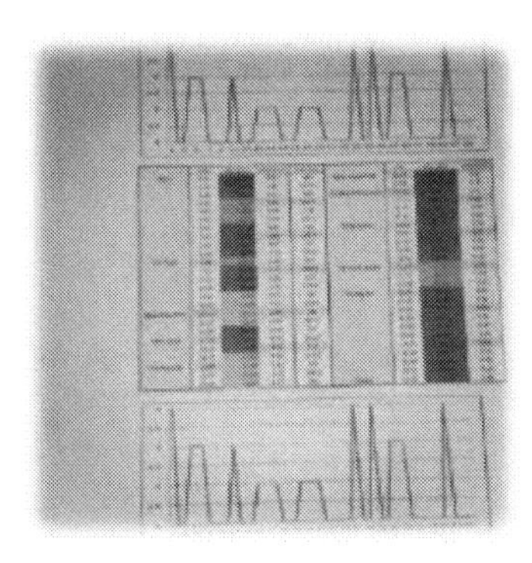

I settled on a run/walk strategy, 25 minutes run, 5 minutes' walk, and the walk period would not only tell me to walk but also to drink and eat. I did this as I knew I would not drink if I continued running, I simply had to slow down in order to think clearly for a few minutes. I planned my race with different pacing for flat, easy, medium and hard inclines. I planned to finish in around 6 hours, it looked fine on paper but as with any project what you plan in theory is not always what happens in practice. I knew this place was hilly, over 2,000 metres of elevation over 30 miles, so I had practiced hills back home and had planned a slow walk pace up hills, but what I hadn't anticipated was the difference in definition of a hill from down South to up ~~North~~ in the Midlands.

Here is the start of my planning, colour coded pace based on incline steepness, I was pretty proud I'd gone to this much trouble, shame I couldn't make the race recce that was held a few weeks earlier which was the same weekend of the Chiltern race as it would have been far more accurate.

The thought of driving all the way there worried not just Sally but also me. I had never driven that far in my life (sad, I know), and I knew that despite planning kit, pace, nutrition, and everything else for this race, the biggest worry was getting not myself to the finish line, my car to the start line. I don't know why I worry so much about the car, it's a 10 year old Ford Fiesta which has barely done 50,000 miles, it's never broken down, and passes it's MOT quite easily every year. I guess I just know that like me, as it ages it will start getting niggles and eventually break down.

I mitigated the risk by booking a hotel; we decided to make a weekend of it so stayed 2 nights. When I say we decided to make a weekend of it, this is kind of true but it also reduced the worry of me hurting myself and not being able to drive home the same day, I don't think Sally would have been too happy with driving all that way home. Our hotel was wonderful, the Roseleigh Hotel, which overlooked the park and lake, just 5 minutes' walk to the start line at Buxton Community School. As I'm so impatient we drove the 240 miles pretty much nonstop, just one short comfort stop, and checked into the hotel. It was more of a large house than a hotel, 5 floors high, our room was on the 5th floor, the owners joked about me climbing a total of 55 steps up to my room after the race; I didn't find this funny!

We took a short walk to find the start line, went for a stroll around the town to catch some fresh air, got frustrated by all the cake shops and tea rooms which I couldn't enjoy until after the race, then settled in for an early night with my usual oversized picnic. This time I also listened to Jacob, who likes half cooked pasta and chickpeas pre-race, I went with a huge portion of pasta mixed with tomato puree, then some crisps as a treat. This was a huge treat, I never eat crisps but keep seeing them at fuel stations so presume they must be an allowed runner's fuel and treated myself. I took in no alcohol that night, I'm learning! The owners also kindly brought up a breakfast for me for the following morning as they knew I'd be setting off well before their breakfast hours.

Morning of the race I totally ignored my carefully planned pre-race breakfast of rice pudding, raisins and banana, instead I tucked into croissants, granola, cheese, fruit and jam. A little stupid really, my eyes are bigger than my belly far too often, but it's a good point to learn from for the future. I pulled on my carefully prepared ultra-vest and the trail shoes which caused me so much pain at the Meon race; I had checked with the organisers in advance that I was making the correct choice this time.

We walked up the road to the start line, I felt quite intimidated, and I know it was just another race but it felt like something far more important to me. The Sky Race brand is well known, the terrain was something I'd never faced before, and the runners all looked so professional and organised. Maybe it was just my eyes deceiving me though, perhaps because I saw this as my number one goal for the year I was just taking things too seriously? I was a little nervous, but also very excited, I may have mentioned it before but I'd read these two feelings are the same, the difference is how you react to the feeling that makes you feel either nervous or excited, so I used this understanding to calm my nerves.

I checked in at registration, got my race number, my chip timer, and also my clip card. I had never had a clip card so was unsure what to do with this, basically you get to unmanned checkpoints which have a unique punch/clip, and you punch holes in the clip card as you go along to show you've done the full route. We also got a map, I was a little worried about the route as it was very new territory for me, but I knew the route was well marked as I'd checked in advance but as a backup had also loaded up my bike computer with the route.

I had linked up with a few runners in advance of the race through social media, it was actually more than I realised as during the race I met quite a few of them. My one big regret from this race is not getting to meet them better either before or after the race, people like Matthew Thompson, Damon

Wheatley, and Scott Berry. I would say this is something I would look back on and wish I'd done better in this race, before the race I was simply too nervous, after the race I was just relieved, but moments like this don't happen often so I need to make more of an effort in future.

As we walked up the road to the start line I got talking to other athletes, one in particular was called Jason Atkins, he was a local runner from Leek who I found out had run many ultras and marathons in the past. This race, he joked, was his birthday present to himself. I don't think this was a joke, I'd done the same last year at the Stort30 (which was exactly one year ago to the day that I'm writing this chapter – 27th October). We were both aiming for around 6 hrs finish time, my aim was probably more optimistic than his, so I saw this as an opportunity to run with someone local who could guide me around the course. Jason agreed to run/walk with me for the race, once he'd done this I started to mention my history, injured legs, passing out, poor pacing, etc., not that I was trying to put him off, more so I prepared my excuses if I slowed him down ☺ (Jason is in the picture here, in the blue next to me)

We all queued up at the start line, a brief final few words from the organisers, and we were off around a field and straight up a hill and into yet another bottleneck situation. I know I complained about these in previous chapters, but since I had no idea what I had to come I was quite happy to slow down and continue talking to Jason here. The hill headed up through some woodland then into clearer ground where we could all spread out, continuing up to a tower with a bagpipe player stood at the top (you don't hear one for years, then two come along in the same year - they had a bagpipe player at the Trionium Munro as well).

From this point we headed back down hill, through the woods, back up again, and into what felt like the wilderness to me. Miles and miles of land, no roads, no houses, no shops, just beautiful countryside which I rapidly found out had large patches of boggy areas. When I decided to start trail races, and then to move to ultra-marathons, I was seduced by the pictures of wonderful trails in the USA, clear blue sky, sun shining, lakes, canyons, and runners looking super cool in their kit, this was my idea of what Sky running was; stupid me. If I had been told in advance the trails in the UK are not always like this, and the conditions tend to get slightly worse the further North you head, I may have reconsidered, the thought of getting wet, dirty and cold reminds me of days at school cross country and rugby (I loved rugby, but that was because I was pretty good at it, I'm not so good at running). Now here I was, barely half an hour into a race, what was to be quite a long time ahead of me to run, and I was ankle deep in mud. My shoes were not waterproof, I was tiptoeing my way to try to pretend I was lighter on my feet than I am so as to not sink further but the runners ahead kindly making the ground even softer than before, I was soaked and covered in mud already. This is the reality of running trails in the UK, you will not often cross the line with a great tan and clean clothes, don't be fooled like I was. I know I'd run races before with similar conditions, difference here was I knew the race was going to be tougher than any other, I had far longer to "enjoy" these conditions.

I've said before the people in ultramarathons and trail races are always so friendly, this was no exception. As I made my way through this boggy patch I got speaking to even more runners, it was at the point I got a shout from behind then got introduced to another social media contact called Berty Bethell – the brother of one of the organisers (Forest) and who also had another brother who was a great runner (Dave). This was Berty's first Ultramarathon, he's a fairly chunky fella like me, very friendly, and he'd prepared the week before the race by going on holiday to Egypt. He lives in the area and was obviously far more tolerant of the weather, he was running in clothes I'd maybe consider in the middle of the summer sun or if I'd accidently forgotten my PE kit, shorts and vest. It turned out I was more the exception, I was wrapped up as if I was one of the Egyptian mummies Berty may have seen on his holiday whereas many others were dressed up like Berty, even the women. I made myself feel better by convincing myself I needed the warmth because of my Raynaud's and also to keep my damaged leg warm. As the race progressed Berty would dart off ahead, then Jason and I would catch him, chat, then overtake him, we seemed to do this from start to finish.

I could write this chapter for many, many, more pages, my blog entry was far too long (almost a book on its own), so I will summarise the rest of the journey.

The race was awesome; we followed all kinds of terrain, it wasn't all muddy. I felt like an explorer, a little like one of the characters I'd played out on my PS2 during my younger years in games like Call of Duty or Far Cry. We went up and down the steepest hills I'd ever encountered, we went through what I think could be classed a quarries, through fields surrounded by wonderful hand built flint walls, past the second highest pub in the UK (Cat and Fiddle), more forests, rivers, and we had cow muck to tread through. We also had sun, warmth, we had rain, and we had wind, the weather changed so much as we went through different landscapes. I ran, I walked, I held people up as we went up and down narrow paths a lot, so sorry for that, I was being careful preserving my damaged leg. I felt like an explorer, not knowing what was up ahead, no idea where I was heading, just following route markings, running in small groups, and basically having what felt like was a great day out with friends.

We ran for a while with a guy I met on Strava called Harry G Vehicle, I found out his name is Gary, not Harry, but I don't know the story behind this. He was one of those poor sods who I held up, firstly along a patch called the Roaches. Short story on this, and a good learning point for me, was that I decided before the race to try gel insoles in my shoes, never having used them before. Reason for this was simply for comfort as the blisters and toenails from the Meon race were still painful, but as I was running I get feeling them moving. As they slipped, one of them edged up and out of my shoes, eventually flapping about behind my heel. This was really annoying, I really couldn't be bothered to put it back in, so I pulled it out and since Harry/Gary was right behind me I passed my insole to him and asked him to slip it into the back of my hydration pack. It wasn't much longer before the other did the same, Harry wasn't behind me and I wasn't going to stop to put it in my bag myself (Jason was up ahead, but still with me at this point), so I slipped this gel insole into the front of my pants. God knows why I did this, I should have just binned it as I've never used them since, but I ran the rest of the race, probably 4+ hrs, with this thing padding out my pants, slightly uncomfortable but also slightly flattering.

Above: Harry, Jason & I, that's Harry getting a good leg stretch at a checkpoint

Another thank you to Kirsty-Jane Birch and her friend Stephanie who kept me company. Both are local girls, also from the Leek area where Jason was from, and dead friendly. I think Kirsty knew me from social media, they said hello as they caught up with us, I introduced myself and Jason, and we seemed to run together for most of the race. I'm sure it was Stephanie's first Ultra-marathon; I know it wasn't Kirsty's, but both were fabulous runners, so good they could run and talk non-stop, sometimes even running while on their phones. I know running is about using oxygen as efficiently as possible, they certainly broke all the rules here. They were also running in these things called skorts, I guess these are for women who can't decide what to wear, shorts or a skirt, so they combined the two. I don't understand the need for this, shorts would be fine, but then men are just as bad wearing shorts over Lycra leggings, why do they do this?

I remember one of the girls asking me if the skort made her bum look big, I didn't know what to say here, was it a trick question. If I answered "no" would I get questioned why I was looking at their bums, if I said "yes" would I get a slap? Truth is I couldn't answer the question, I was enjoying their company, and time flew by as we chatted, but I'm more interested in looking at the floor as I trudge up and down hills. I also remember them commenting on my kit choice, yes I was dressed up as if it were the middle of winter, I may have looked an idiot in long lycra pants and arm warmers, but I was comfortable and the arm warmers ended up being a great option as I could roll them up and down as the weather changed. Kirsty and Steph were also very good at embarrassing me when running through puddles, they'd just run through them, I would walk around them. The picture here is a photo of Kirsty and Steph, the cow mess made Steph attractive to flies.

The one other guy I'd like to mention was the old bloke, I can't remember his name, he must have been 60+, and like Berty I seemed to follow him for most of the race, cat and mouse style. Despite his perceived old(ish) age, he would bound down hills like a teenage, zooming past me without a care in the world, then on the flats Jason and myself would catch him, then overtake up the hills. I was to learn he was quite a well-known fell runner, there were many people similar to him in the race, locals who were used to such hills, I was in awe of the ease in which they speed down what I thought were really steep hills. It's a fine art to do this, lots of skill, but also I'd imagine a mental thing, you must have to run with no fear of falling, pretty relaxed, and the stiffer you run, the harder it is. I've read personal development books which encourage you to think like a child to help with creativity, I think this is the running equivalent, run like a child.

What follows is a montage of photos from the race, if you're not inspired to do such a race through either of my books, then I hope these photos will, simply amazing. At the very least go visit the area, great just for hiking (and tea rooms).

The rest of the race went really well, I stuck pretty well to the run/walk (drink) strategy, I still didn't eat or drink everything I took with me but the fuel stations were ace and I made the most of them, including the free Chia Charge flapjacks which were delicious. I certainly did much better than the Chiltern race with my fuel, I don't think I could have done worse really, as a bonus the weather wasn't so warm which helped loads.

I did suffer with my leg a bit, but I was sensible and didn't worry so much about the goal time, deciding that this was maybe a once in a lifetime race for me and what was the point in rushing it, so walked as much as I needed. It turned out my walk pace was actually pretty good uphill, Sally always complains I steam off ahead of her uphill, I did similar in this race. I felt guilty about sometimes leaving Jason behind on the uphill's, I mentioned this to him at one point, but I simply needed to keep moving plus I knew he'd always catch me up downhill, so it worked out fine for us overall. I had one small incident with cramp as I crossed over a wall, but I walked this off relatively easily. Jason also had a few issues with what I think was cramps, I gave him some salt tablets which I was surprised he hadn't tried before, and we also had one small problem getting lost towards the end but luckily my bike computer map saved us, beeping to tell me we were off course and pointing us in the correct direction.

I'm really grateful to Jason, and the others I met, for their company, it made a long race feel so much easier, time flew past. We agreed at the start to run together, and we did from start to pretty much the end, as the title of this book says, "run alone if you want to go fast, run together if you want to go far". If one of us needed to walk, the other slowed, down, we chatted, learnt about each other, had a laugh, and had periods of silence which never felt awkward. Jason had joked this was to be his last ultra, I know since this race he's done shorter races including marathons, but I think he will be tempted to run further again in the future. Whether this temptation is enough to actually enter another ultra who knows, he has run more than me and further than me so he has nothing to prove, just plenty more to experience. I bet he has some awesome stories which would make a great book.

We got to about a mile out from the finish line, it was downhill all the way, and we were on track to finish in around 7 hours. I thought of poor Sally waiting at the finish line, worrying about me after the last race and wondering where I was as I'd said I'd finish between 6 and 7 hours. I didn't want to worry her further, even if it were to only give her a minute less of worry, so I checked Jason was happy with me running on, and then surprisingly managed to sprint to the finish line and finished in 6 hr 57 minutes, 76th out of 130. I felt really good as I crossed, fresh enough to continue running further, no cramps, no pains in my feet, even my nuts weren't sore after the insole rubbing me up for many miles. I know I could have ran this harder, who knows if I had I may have finished faster, but also I may not have finished at all. I'm glad I used the strategy I took on the day as I finished well which is more important, I guess that's the sign of a better prepared race, with maybe less of an emphasis on racing and more on enjoyment. The medal was great, but even better was the T-shirt I got, so comfortable, good quality, I'm now very proud to wear it in the gym. Jason finished shortly after, Kirsty and Steph finished in front of us.

Another good sign was my appetite; it was ready to demolish the generous food table waiting at the end. They had hot drinks, soup, bread, loads of cake, and plenty more. My mind wasn't thinking too straight at this point, I remember the lady serving mentioning they had cakes with strawberries, and also tomato soup, so I asked for strawberry soup. They also had showers available which was appreciated, especially by the owner of the hotel where I was staying at as the house rules warned me she didn't want muddy shoes through her house. My trainers, which I'd only worn 3 times but had worked fine in this race, had a tear in the side probably from the rocks, so I retired them at the finish line by dumping in a bin. This was a shame really as the soles were still brand new, but as my experience was growing I also started to appreciate the need for better quality shoes for similar races in the future.

Biggest learning point from this race, ashamed to say it again but it's the shoe choice. Not specifically the shoes, even though they ripped they served me well on the day, but those insoles were a pain in the backside. Sally did point out to me after I'd put them in upside down, I thought the gel side which was a little sticky was so me feet stuck well to them, it turned out it was so the insole stuck to the shoe, plus I should have taken out the original insole from the shoes (I'd left them in, and then put the gel insoles on top of them), in hindsight I really didn't need them. The other learning points were the hills, I can't use my leg as an excuse forever, it either heals and I get more confident at them, or it continues to hurt and I either accept I slow down or pick shorter/less hilly races, something I'd work on at a future race. I also learnt that it's worth the effort to at least plan your race, if not recce it, in advance. I had done well on this last point, even wrote down key milestones on my arm to stick to the plan and the words "drink you idiot" on my hand, shame my arm warmers and the sweat rubbed that off before we got to the top of the first hill.

I am so glad I entered this race, I would never have visited such a nice part of the UK, would not have met some wonderful people, would not have had such a great day out, and possibly without entering it would not have pushed myself so hard to recover from last year's injury. I wish I'd spent more time in the area, met with more people I have got to know as they were so friendly, maybe another time.

This was the highlight of my running career for sure and wins my award for "Best Experience of the Year". I cancelled my entry to the Brecon Beacon 50 mile event after this, I was disappointed to do this but felt it best to not push my leg any harder, I was also not in need of pushing my mind any harder in a running race, the Sky race had given me all I needed for the time being. This turned out to be an excellent decision for someone else called Barden Davis. Barden had raced the Brecon event the previous year but missed out on getting a place this year; as I said it fills up really quickly, so when I asked if anyone wanted my place he grabbed it. The saying goes "one man's loss is another man's gain" and this was certainly true as Barden won the race, 50 miles in under 7 hours in appalling weather. I don't know Barden, but I'm so pleased for him.

A final special thank you to the wonderful volunteers who looked after us all so well at the fuel stations, as they have done on all the other races I've run – a race wouldn't happen without you all.

## A free race series – Parkrun (various dates)

Parkrun's are free, weekly 5k runs, held on a Saturday at 9am in many places across the work, the attendance is huge – I've run with anything from 100 to 500 people in these events.

Last year I ran one Parkrun event in Southsea; this was the day before the Isle of Wight half marathon and was intended as a last leg loosener before the race. Needless to say I totally ignored the race the next day and ended up racing the full 5k, finishing just outside a sub 20 minute time, which was okay but I was slightly disappointed as I'd regularly breaking 20 minutes on a treadmill at that point, even breaking 19 minutes on one occasion.

I didn't run any further Park runs in 2014, and hadn't really bothered about speed in 2015, but then in August my leg was slowly healing but not as quickly as I liked, so I decided to try something different and do some fast running.

When I was bodybuilding and powerlifting I got the occasional injury, usually a tight back caused through lack of stretching, and I would try resting to recover. I quickly found out that this did nothing for me, the soreness stayed with me no matter what I did, so I decided to "Flip It" (search Amazon for a book by the same name, worth a read), and went back to the gym and trained harder and heavier than before. This may sound stupid, a doctor would have just told me to continue resting just as they told me to rest my leg at the start of this year, but to me it made more sense that in order to strengthen a weak point, it's better to train it, not rest it. Of course if the injury was so serious I would never have done this, but for an ache, a niggle, or just a pain, whatever you want to call it, it was worth a shot. This method served me well on numerous occasions in the past so I decided to do the same for running, strengthen the weakness in my leg, which I thought may help the fast twitch muscle fibres; the slow twitch were getting strengthened through the slower runs. Parkrun was the solution to this, we have numerous courses local to me over various kinds of courses, plus it gave me a good reason to meet up with friends who also ran these.

In 2015 I ran Parkruns in Southsea (fastest, flat along the seafront, out and back, usually with a stiff breeze in your face with the bonus of a swim in the sea afterward), Queen Elizabeth Country Park (slowest, a trail loop, reasonable elevation gain), and also the Havant course (medium, also a trail loop, less incline than QE, but one steep decline and a gradual incline).

I'm not going to give you a blow by blow account of each Parkrun I did, below are some of my stats, but I found they really helped strengthen up my leg, it certainly started feeling better both mentally and physically as I pushed myself on these courses, competing against not only myself but also against others which made a change to my race purpose.

Southsea Parkrun – 9 runs, best position 14th, fastest run 20:06, slowest 21:38

Havant Parkrun – 4 runs, best position 13th, fastest 21:37, slowest 22:29

Queen Elizabeth Parkrun – 2 runs, best position 9th, fastest 22:12, slowest 22:26

So far this year I haven't managed to get back to the speed I had last year, reasons may be that apart from Parkrun I've not really done any speed work such as intervals, I'm also heavier, and am still very tight in my glutes and hamstrings, but looking on the bright side one thing I have improved on is pacing. When I did my first 5k this year I did the usual, setting off way too hard and then hanging on at the end. Now I am slowing down at the start, finishing stronger, and achieving a negative split which I've been told is the correct strategy for running. The issue I have with this is overall I'm still faster setting off like a fool and finishing slow, but I'm going to stick with it and see what happens. This year I have broken 20 minutes on a treadmill 5k (just), so I have it in me, I just need to practice.

These races also gave me the chance to meet up with friends, sometimes encouraging friendly competition during the race, often a chat at the end; it's always a lot of fun running with others even in short races.

A few names stick out here, George Garrett and Simon Boreham were my running buddies at Southsea, and we'd often finish within a minute of each other, all of us had a similar goal of breaking

20 minutes. George is the only one to do this so far in 2015, but that only inspires me and Simon to try harder.

Another guy is Richard Johnstone (also known by the surname Lacock), who is a South African that has lived in the UK for many years now. Richard is an awesome ultra-runner who is just as good at 5k's, he's run in many countries at many distances, he makes things look so easy when I watch him which is probably why he's so good – he doesn't waste energy pulling stupid faces like I do, or running junk miles (he's been injured quite a lot like me this year, but has been way more patient than me in recovery). I would watch Richard's style and try to learn from it, usually just for the first few hundred metres before he'd disappear into the distance, but it's helped a lot.

Another runner I met was Phil Branigan. I'd got to know Phil over social media but never met him. One day, while running on the return home leg of the Southsea Parkrun, coming towards me was a familiar face, waving and saying "hello". I instantly recognised Phil and his smiling face and so I waited for him at the finish line. I had the pleasure of having a swim in the Solent and a chat with him and his friend, Phillip Hale. It turned out they were on a road trip to find a different Parkrun to do and decided to turn up at Southsea, Phil knew I ran this one as well and it was just good timing that we all turned up on the same day. Despite my obsession with getting sub 20 again, meeting Phil was a highlight from the Parkruns this year, a guy who runs a lot of races for good causes, always seeming to have fun, running with a smile. When I asked him if he was happy to have a mention in this book he commented he and his friends were "just Parkrun tourists from different clubs in Basingstoke". I think he undersells this, Phil epitomises what Parkrun is all about, runners having fun, running in new places, making friends, challenging yourself and others to improve.

There must be many great Parkrun stories from runners across the world; it would make a great book in itself. It's so inclusive; it's free so no excuses, you turn up as you wish so no commitment or pressure. I've managed to lap some people in races and yet they still seem to be having a great time. I've just as easily been overtaken by people pushing children in prams; the kids seem to enjoy this even when their buggy is being pushed hard over trails and up/down hills. I've watched people running with and being toward by their dogs, I've been beaten and have also enjoyed beating juniors, and recently I saw a guy in his 80's run his first Parkrun. It goes to prove, you're never too young, old, unfit, out of time, to get fit and healthy.

So over the last 18 months I've moved away from the faster, shorter races because I felt they were less fun and also didn't help my lack of patience. It was as I became more experienced over these Parkruns and met more people that I began to change my mind about this. Sure, the 5k is probably more intense than 50k (some are lucky enough to race a 50k, I'm not one of those), and if you're running it for the fastest time then you're probably in no mood to talk to others, but this needn't be the case. To run flat out every week is challenging on the body (even more so as you get older), so it's good to have slower weeks (or even become a volunteer marshal), where you practice pacing, breathing, or maybe even a pacer for someone else. Even if you run hard, it's only 20 minutes, I found plenty of time to catch up with friends before and after the race, even just talking to strangers. Maybe it was just my ego changing, previously I wanted to take part in niche events and to do something extra-ordinary, not ordinary, but now I've done some of those I could now tick that box I started finding enjoyment and challenges in other things. Perhaps this is linked back to a short attention span, I just wanted to do something new again?

If you're interested in Parkrun just search the net, it's easy to find, easy to sign up, once you've signed up there's no commitment, hey also now hold junior Park runs.

To end this section I wanted to also mention the Great Run Local series, very similar to Parkrun. This is a UK event which is a subset of the Great Run series of longer national events (think Great North Run, Great South Run, etc.). Just like Parkrun this is a 5k race, but they also have 2k options (so a shorter race on the same day), unlike Parkrun these events are not held on the same day/same time across the country. This series is still quite small, it seems to have been running in the central and northern areas of the UK for a while, we recently had one started local to myself, so I signed up for free via their website, got my timing bracelet (no paper barcode needed like Parkrun), and have run one so far – it had a much smaller attendance than Parkrun, probably a good thing as the course was quite tight, but was just as enjoyable. Search the net for more info "Great Run Local".

I'm going to continue with these events, the have shown me it's possible to compete whilst also having fun, to sometimes slow down and run smarter, and to be inspired by a whole new group of runners.

## What do I prefer, running or cycling? – Portsmouth Duathlon (06/09)

The Peak Sky race was complete, I didn't want to ruin it by entered another "A" race for 2015 (that would have made the Sky race my "B" race), so I went in search of a different challenge.

I had enjoyed running, found a love for cycling, and was also now competing in the Parkrun's, so I wanted to do something to pull all this together. I had friends who competed in triathlons and ironman events, but I didn't have the time to practice swimming (I can swim, but the front crawl technique needs practice), so I decided to find a duathlon to do instead.

I signed up for this race on 12th August, shortly after finishing the Sky race, I figured there was very little I needed to do to get ready for it, it was just a 5k run, 40k bike, 10k run, I'd managed all of those easily during the year, I just needed to do them one after the other now.

My friend George warned me of two things to look out for in a duathlon, wobbly leg syndrome (coming off the bike and moving to the second run can feel strange) and smooth transitions between run to bike and back again.

For the wobbly leg syndrome I did a few sessions where I'd switch between bike and running, either outside or in the gym. It was a strange feeling, but I wouldn't say it caused me any worries, with the long distance running I'm used to have numb feelings in my run later in the race, this was no worse really.

For the transitions, I didn't practice at all; my bike/run training sessions would involve me getting home on my bike, putting it in the garage, maybe going to the toilet, having a quick drink, changing my trainers, and then off for the run, not exactly a slick transition. I didn't worry about this as I figured I wouldn't be competing for top spot plus the thought of practicing something which would save me seconds in the race was pretty pointless when there was the opportunity to save far more by practicing cycling and running harder, faster, and smarter.

So with a few weeks of practice, treating my bike to a service and myself to a tri-suit, I turned up on the day not really knowing what to expect.

The race was part of the Portsmouth Triathlon weekend, organised by the local council. The duathlon hadn't really been advertised, it was hidden under the triathlon details, no information was sent out in advance, the website even said things like race briefing videos would be online a few days before, they never were.

On the day first impressions it looked really good, a huge transition area, and lots of people, quite professional really. But then the duathletes were called and we gathered together and it was a little disappointing, there were less than 20 of us taking part, the triathlons (sprint and Olympic) had 100's. I don't think this is because duathlons are not popular, I think it was purely down to the poor advertising, I had friends who do duathlons tell me they hadn't even noticed it was taking part. This was pretty poor by the organisers really but I was there, it had cost quite a lot to enter, so I was going to make the most of it.

The start was a shambles, we were queued up at 7am, ready to start the 5k leg, but we had to wait to start with the triathletes who were running late with their briefings. It was a brisk morning, we were getting cold, and 15 minutes late we set off along what was pretty much the same route as the Southsea Parkrun. Unlike the Parkrun, this 5k was devoid of many marshals and no atmosphere. We ran past a couple of marshals stood together halfway on the outward leg (it was an out and back run), but at the turnaround point there was just a cone on the pavement, no one stood with it, and we headed back. This was really poor, anyone could have moved that cone, and thankfully it was so early in the morning that kids were not around to do this.

I finished the 5k in around 21 ½ minutes, really trying to pace myself well and not setting off like an idiot. My Parkrun practice paid off, I did a perfect negative split, 7:04, 7:01, 6:56 miles, I was really happy with this.

The first transition went well; whipped off my running trainers, put my cycling shoes which had a Velcro fastener, helmet on, grabbed bike, ran across a fairly muddy field, and onto 6 laps of Southsea seafront for the 40k bike ride. This was a totally flat course, quite a few corners, I wasn't really used to cycling such courses, flat and fast was not really something I looked forward to as like running I prefer the challenge of a hill and motivation of the countryside. I had tri-bars on my bike so tucked into position and just cycled hard, stretching my back every now and again as it tightened up. This section was incredibly boring, just going around and around, there were not that many cyclists around as the triathlon was still finishing the swimming leg.

At around lap 4 the triathletes started to keep us company, there were a mixture of amateurs (don't mean to be disrespectful here, but many were on mountain bikes), and then there were the supermen/women on their tri-bikes (stealth bikes) zooming around which had an awesome "whirring" noise from their slick wheels and the attached discs slicing through the air. I managed quite a steady pace in the bike section, around 20 mph, finishing in around 1 ¼ hours, and then had to transition for the final 10k run.

I had a few problems on this transition, having been stuck in the cycle position for so long my Raynaud's had kicked in pretty hard. My feet and hands were so numb, I fumbled about trying to tie up my shoes laces while Sally looked on through the fencing, unable to help me. After 3 attempts I go the laces tied and set off on the 10k run, out and back in the opposite direction along the seafront to the 5k race, 2 laps in total.

I was actually feeling fairly fresh for this last section, admittedly I had taken a long time to do that last transition so caught my breath back quite a lot. I was busting for the loo by this stage, leaning forwards in a fixed position on the bike, pressing on my bladder, was not a comfortable position, but with the tri-suit on there was no way I could quickly dart into a bush or a public toilet for a comfort stop without losing a lot of time and momentum. I'm not sure what others do in this circumstance, do you just wet yourself, or are you just more experienced and drink less than I did? I don't know what the ideal solution is but on this occasion I simply held on until the end. Despite having a well-known nutrition brand on site, this was only on this leg of the race that the organisers supplied and refreshments, I thought this was really poor given the entrance fee which was over £50; maybe we are just spoilt on running races though? The fuel on this last leg was just one station at 2.5km (so we passed it twice, once each lap), and all it had was water. Due to me needing a pee I ignored this table on the first lap, and on the second I just grabbed a cup and chucked the water over me to cool down and hydrate.

The 10k went fine, nothing outstanding, I stuck to my sensible splits plan and worried less about finishing fast, I even was more than happy to let someone run past me and to not react by trying to keep up with them. My finish time was 45m 14s, my first mile was a little fast at 7m3s, but apart from that I didn't really deviate much from my 7m30s/mile plan, fastest was 7m25, slowest 7m48.

I crossed the line with an overall time of 2h 26m 24s, placed 5th overall, got my medal and a goodie bag which contained nothing more than a load a flyers for other events. This event is the winner of my "biggest anti-climax" reward, I didn't feel a wave of emotion come over afterwards, I chatted to others who had taken part and they also agreed, but also told me this wasn't typical of other duathlons they had taken part in it so maybe I will do others in the future (I now have a tri-suit, I have to find a reason to justify having bought it).

I had no cramps, no injuries, and felt pretty fresh after this race. I think the training went well, my relaxed attitude towards the race helped, my diet leading up to it was terrible though; Sally and I had a fabulous afternoon tea a couple of days before the event, not what you'd call an athlete's diet but hugely motivating. I did find myself stiffening up in the days afterwards, especially in the arse and legs department, I think the bike ride did this, stuck in that position constantly grinding out fast splits, it was boring but also undeniably intense.

So I would do a duathlon again? Most probably I would.

The plan at the start of 2015 was to enter the Southsea series of duathlons which happens April to June and is not run by the council. There is far better feedback on these, but the injury meant I didn't do this so maybe I can build up to at least one of these races into my training plan for next year. I think a better bike, one which is lighter, more aerodynamic, better gears, will make a huge difference here as well as with any other sportive I do, but then something that is meant to be for fun starts becoming expensive – first the bike, then a new tri-suit, trainers, fuel, and then what next, wet-suit? Not only does this cost so much money, it means you generalise rather than specialise, and on top of that there's finding time to do training. Maybe the best route is to specialise in just the most easily accessible event which is running as I can do this anywhere, and do anything else as cross training? Another thing I learnt after this race was that you can buy things called bungee laces; these are popular with triathletes due to the problems I encountered with my laces at transition. I had used them before with trail shoes but these were included with the shoes, I didn't realise you could buy them, so maybe a cheap, but wise, investment for the future.

## Wrong course, right medal, going for Gold – Southern Sportive (13/09)

SouthernSportive.com ROAD CYCLING EVENTS

Home | News | Enter Events | Results Archive | What is a Cyclosportive? | About Us | Contact Us

Reading | South Downs | Cranleigh | Chilterns 24 Apr | Swindon 15 May | Reigate 3 Jul | South Downs | South Downs 11 Sep | Henley 17 Sep | Cotswolds 9 Oct

I'd completed the Skyrace, my first sportive, and also a duathlon, but it was still only September and I still had the drive inside of me to do something else new, to push myself harder and try something new. I had completed 2 bike sportives this year, both of those I really enjoyed yet at the end wished I'd taken up the challenge of the longer 100 mile/161 km option. 100 miles sounds huge to me, whether I'm comparing to anything I've run before, or even a distance I'd cover in my car, to me 100 miles means twice the risk of a puncture versus a 50 mile ride, twice the time on a painful saddle, but also twice the opportunity to test myself and see new places, so 2 days before the start day I entered this race. This was to be my longest time on the saddle, my further distance cycled, my highest elevation ever, 3 firsts in one go, a great way to start winding down my year.

Apart from some short rides of 20 mile or less I hadn't done much cycling, I had concentrated my time on running in preparation for the Skyrace, but I felt confident I could get around the course in one piece. The worst thing about cycling is the saddle sore, I wear padded cycling shorts, I won't use a padded saddle though, and I always suffer after. Perhaps with more training you build toughened skin in your bum cheeks or just get used to this? As I mentioned in a previous chapter, I still have fairly big, strong legs from the bodybuilding days, this also helps with the cycling, it's a weakness for running (especially longer distances), but great when you're trying to put power through the pedals. My bodyweight probably is less of a problem when cycling, it slows me down on flats and makes uphill harder, but then downhill it speeds me up despite me forever twitching on my brakes.

This race was fairly local, starting about 15 miles away in Petersfield, heading east through the South Downs national park, and then looping back, heading a little further west, and back to the start point. Despite it being local there were many areas I had never visited so I uploaded the map into my bike computer, even if I didn't need it for route finding it would be useful to give me an indication of how far I'd gone on a distance and elevation basis. This race was the first I'd entered that had gold, silver, bronze, and then a no medal, finishing zones which I quite liked as gave me a goal to aim at. I figured my bike computer would give me an indication of my finishing time to keep me aware throughout the race of my podium position, and thanks to a challenge from my friend George Garrett, I accepted the challenge of going for the gold medal time of something like 5hr55m.

Sally drove me up to the start line and helped me get ready. It was a fairly social atmosphere at the start, more than previous races, I found a few dead friendly cyclists who would chat away to me. There were also the club cyclists with their nice bikes and co-ordinated clothing who stuck together, and then there were the nervous first timers who possibly were doing the shorter options just as I had done earlier in the year.

We lined up on a queue at the start line, had our race briefing, and then set off in waves of about 20, a few minutes apart. As Sally stood to the side watching me edge forwards, I turned on my bike computer to obtain a signal and get ready. I looked over at Sally a little nervous at this point, to my shock I'd uploaded the wrong course, I had the shortest distance instead of the longest distance, maybe this was fate telling me not to do the longer option, maybe I was just rushing my preparation due to the last minute entry? Either way I had no choice, I could still use the computer, I would know things like time elapsed, speed, elevation, distance, but I wouldn't have the course on the screen to warn me of things like sharp corner ahead, big hill ahead, etc. No time to worry, I set off with my group of riders, along a main road, and straight over a deep pothole. For once I couldn't moan about my bike here, it's like a tank compared to many other bikes around me on the day, but it has its benefits and took on the pothole head on. Whilst a carbon bike may have suffered damage over such a hole, my bike absorbed it well, but my drink bottle which was fairly lose in its cage, popped out onto the road due to the heavy impact. Some cyclists behind me managed to avoid it as it rolled across the road, unfortunately a car didn't and rode straight over it, popping the top off the bottle and my drink ending up all over the road, the lid surviving but damaged. Luckily I had 2 bottles on my bike and there were 3 fuel stops along the way, but again this had me wondering if it were a warning of things to come. They say things happen in 3's, so perhaps the dreaded puncture was next?

I collected my bottle; composed myself, and then set off to try catching the group I was with, eventually managing to catch the back markers. I got talking to a few cyclists along the way, comparing stories of previous races as we cycled, but I wouldn't say the conversations were memorable, just polite chat then taking the hint to shut up and move on. There were also the odd cyclists who annoyed me, some I would class as "wannabe elites" who would shoot up behind us shouting "coming through" or "make way", and then there were the club cyclists who would ride abreast of each other, blocking traffic and other cyclists. Drivers often moan about cyclists, almost as much as cyclists moaning about drivers, I can understand the reasons from both sides, some cyclists don't really help themselves though.

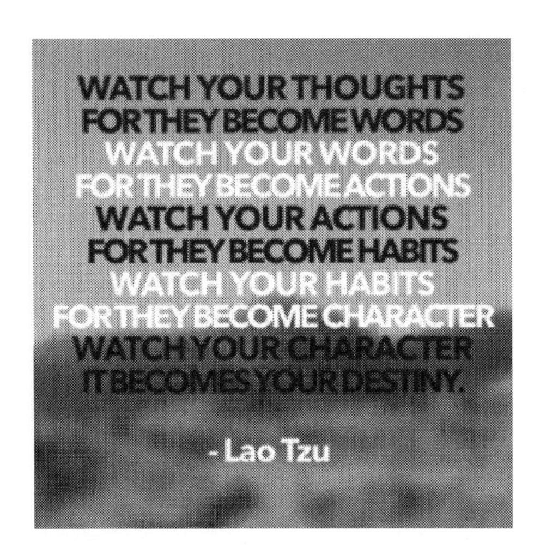


The ride overall was fantastic, a mixture of hills (around 2000 metres or 7000 feet of elevation in total) and quiet country roads. I did ride most of it in silence, it sometimes felt like the longest ride ever (well it was, but it was worse in silent), yet was also quite enjoyable to have some peace and quiet, good contemplation time. I kept track of various data points, trying to work out whether I'd finish in the gold medal time. My goal was slowly slipping away, but then I used some of the inner thinking I'd read about to understand why this gold medal was falling away.

I have said in previous chapters how I was running less to compete, and more to experience, and I realised this was now happening in the bike race. I think this quote sums up what was happening both for running and in my life in general, I was losing my competitive streak and finding it difficult to turn it back on.

Whilst I wanted to compete and go for gold, I was also enjoying the ride, spending a lot of time admiring the views and loving the fresh air, but ultimately not really paying enough attention to the goal. If I had uploaded the right course this would have been less of a problem, the computer would have been making me constantly aware of predicted finish time, I would have been conscious rather than sub-conscious of this.

As the race went on the field of cyclists thinned out more and more, I could go for miles and not see anyone, I began thinking harder and harder about what was going on. I thought about previous rides I'd done, the speeds I knew I was capable of, and began calculating in my head if I got close to those speeds would I get my gold medal finishing time. It was close, but if I picked up to around 20 mph then I would just make it, only problem was that because of the lack of course in my Garmin I had no idea what the elevation profile looked like so I'd have to accept I'd slow down going up, and try making up time on the way down. I love maths; I really enjoyed it at school and still find mental arithmetic a great way to relax. I think this has lead me to a small case of OCD with numbers, I find myself trying to finish runs on whole numbers, preferably also with a time which ends .00. I don't just do this when exercising, for example with the volume on my home TV where I insist on the volume being at 22 which is one of my favourite numbers, I can't set it at 23 as this has no significance to me, 21 is doable at a push as it's the date of my birthday.

For the first time in what felt like a long time I fixated my mind on a finishing time, it was possible I knew it; I just had to focus and push myself hard. A person is like a machine, it's not easy to switch between tasks (which is why multi-tasking at work is so inefficient), and even harder to switch between mind sets (to experience a race versus to compete in a race). I read once that even if you move from one task to a different task, the mind takes around 30 minutes to catch up, this is definitely true. In factories they machine production lines and machines productivity, machine changeover is a key bottleneck (search SMED), and they work hard to reduce the number of and time to complete machine changeovers. Think also of Formula One cars, the speed of the car is so important during 90% of the race, but the wheel changeover is a key differentiator between winning and losing, they practice and improve this religiously.

I found I was really enjoyed this challenge, I was on my own, analysing every bit of my machine. By the word machine I mean my head and how it was thinking (conscious or sub-conscious), my seating position (in or out of saddle, apparently in saddle is better, my natural inclination is out of saddle so I kept correcting it), I was even analysing my food position on the pedal (when you push down do you have your heal higher or lower than your toe, I've still not worked out which is best). I kept an eye on the stats on my Garmin (not easy, the screen is not always so clear), and the goal which had been slipping away from me was coming back in sight.

At one point during this stage I remember pushing hard on a small incline, probably pulling one of my worst maximum effort facial expressions, and I passed a field of cows that started mooing at me. I know they do this all the time as a warning to stay away, but I wasn't thinking too clearly at that point, so I started shouting at them something along the lines of "who the f#ck are you laughing at" and "I'm trying as hard as a can, give me a break". I sometimes get quite emotional in races, time alone, lack of energy, and tiredness, all do funny things to your brain (as was obvious on the Chiltern race with the dehydration), I felt like crying at this point as for the first time in a while I was fixated on winning. When I run and try to enjoy races I use moments like this to try relaxing, almost meditate while moving, but now I was competing and my old aggressive side started to peak its ugly head out. Thank god I was on my own, I don't like seeing this side of me, I thought it had gone but I guess you can't change who you are.

I was coming towards the end of the race and recognising the route ahead I calculated that I was well on track now for gold medal time. I stupidly started to relax, I was knackered, but I knew I had about 25 minutes to get to the finish line, the route was just straight ahead, back to where we started – weird thing was the bike computer told me I still had further to go distance wise. I assumed this was just a GPS error, computers do make mistakes, so edged closer to the finish line, getting to the point where the bike bottle incident occurred, literally metres away from the end, and then I saw a route marking directing me away from the finish – I thought "what the hell is going on here!" If only that map had uploaded properly I would have seen this well in advance and not relaxed, I would now be in serious danger of missing my goal, I would be a total failure in my eyes and it was my entire fault, so many things I could have done better. Below is a map of my perceived finishing route (black line) and the actual finishing route (blue line). It was 5 hrs 48 minutes when I had to take the right turn, about 8 minutes inside the gold medal time, it turned out that instead of metres to cycle; I still had around 4km to go. The weather all day had been fine, no sun, not hot, by dry, but now the weather reflected how I felt, it clouded over, it started raining, and I felt like crying again, I was emotionally drained.

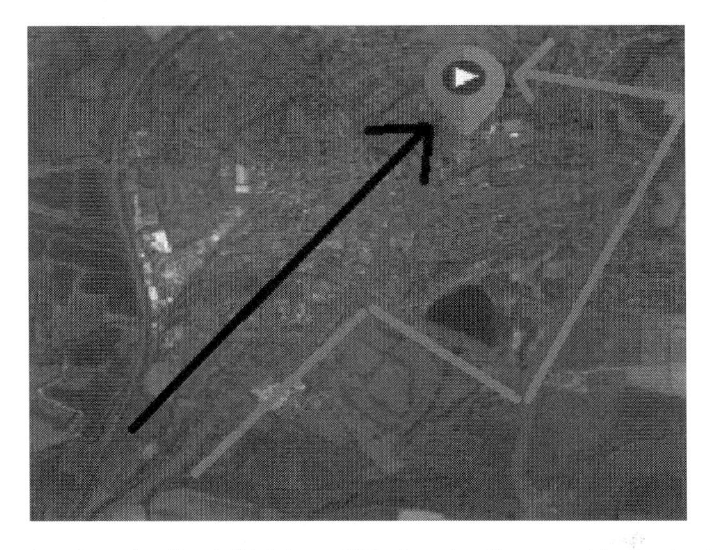

I had no idea where I was heading, I didn't know if I had roads still to cross (the Sunday drivers were out in force by this time, no way would they be going fast, and definitely would not be allowing a cyclist to pull out), but I hadn't given up hope. I pushed so bloody hard at this point, I know my stats don't show great speed, but it was hard on me both mentally and physically. I was practically at the finish line, I came to a roundabout/one way section, and ignoring everything about road safety I shot across this, took a sharp left and crossed the finish line. The gold medal time was 5hr56minutes, my Garmin told me I was 6 seconds outside, and I was gutted, worst still I was alone and for the third time in this race I felt like crying.

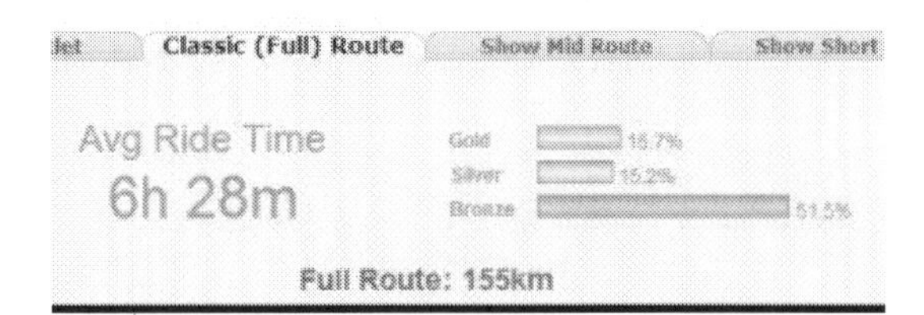


When running people ask the difference between chip and gun time, those who are the back of the field will always have a difference between these. The process goes the gun goes off, the timer starts, but their chip does not start until they cross the timing mat, only once you cross that mat does you own time start. In this race something similar happened, the gun went off; I pressed start on my Garmin, but then had to clip my toes into the pedals, slowly edge forward with the crowd of cyclists ahead of me, and eventually crossed the timing mat. I hadn't thought of this when I ended the race; I was kind of relying on their kindness to give me a Gold medal based on effort. Thankfully I didn't have to rely on this, my chip time was just inside the Gold time, I had won the medal I wanted, under 17% of riders won that gold and I was one of them, in fact more riders received no medal than received the gold medal.

The Peak Sky race was without a doubt my "best experience of the year", but I would say this race wins my award for "biggest achievement of the year". I had drifted from being competitive to almost complacent over the last 12 months or so, just going through the motions and not feeling pressure so much. I would never change the way I ran the Sky race, running it with great company was awesome, if I had run it on my own I could have finished faster, or I could have not finished and injured myself again, who knows, but the goal (especially given how I started the year) was to enjoy and finish it. As mentioned in the Parkrun chapter, I was now starting to find a happy compromise (in statistics it may be called regression to the norm), where I could compete and find happiness.

Sally was not there at the finish line for me that day, I think this was the first time ever, but it was my choice, she had things she wanted to do at our allotment, so I phoned her up and she came to collect me. I replayed this chapter to her blow for blow; if I were driving I probably would have driven the route so she could have been bored by my drivel even more.

Learning points from this race, I think the saying in the army goes "piss poor preparation produces poor performance", it was certainly true here. Another thing I learnt after uploading my race details, don't waste time at fuel stations, I think I was static for around 20 minutes in total while filling my face, I could have finished the race in a more relaxed state if I'd improved on this point.

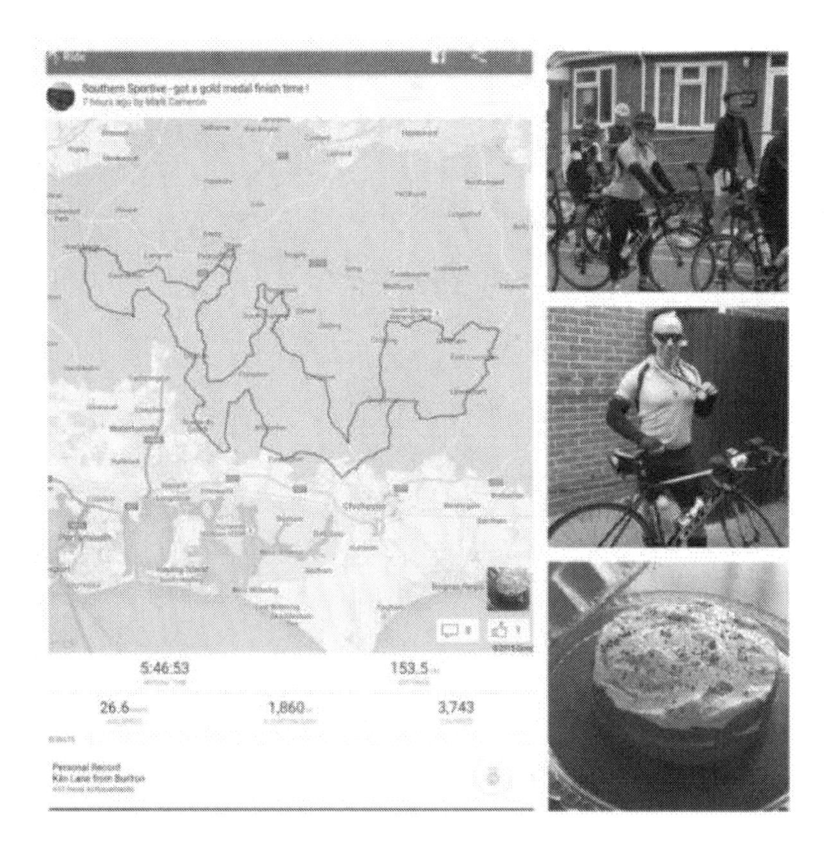
5:46:53
153.5
26.6
1,860
3,743

Here you can see the difference between the 10 miles where I acknowledged my slowdown

| | Total time | | Moving Time | | Elevation +/- | | Speed |
|---|---|---|---|---|---|---|---|
| 67 | 3:29.6 | 4:09:15 | 3:30 | 1.61 | 19 | 15 | 27.6 |
| 68 | 3:13.1 | 4:12:28 | 3:12 | 1.61 | 9 | 16 | 30.0 |
| 69 | 4:29.7 | 4:16:58 | 4:26 | 1.61 | 31 | 0 | 21.5 |
| 70 | 3:37.9 | 4:20:36 | 3:39 | 1.61 | 15 | 26 | 26.6 |
| 71 | 3:30.5 | 4:24:06 | 3:30 | 1.61 | 8 | 5 | 27.5 |
| 72 | 3:45.2 | 4:27:52 | 3:46 | 1.61 | 15 | 2 | 25.7 |
| 73 | 4:28.7 | 4:32:20 | 4:28 | 1.61 | 34 | 9 | 21.6 |
| 74 | 5:08.9 | 4:37:29 | 5:09 | 1.61 | 57 | 13 | 18.8 |
| 75 | 7:27.4 | 4:44:57 | 7:23 | 1.61 | 52 | 0 | 12.9 |
| 76 | 5:15.8 | 4:50:12 | 5:13 | 1.61 | 54 | 10 | 18.3 |

And the final 10 miles where I got my arse in gear and started pushing a little harder

| | | | | | | | |
|---|---|---|---|---|---|---|---|
| 90 | 3:17.6 | 5:39:21 | 3:17 | 1.61 | 11 | 30 | 29.3 |
| 91 | 3:21.7 | 5:42:42 | 3:23 | 1.61 | 4 | 13 | 28.7 |
| 92 | 3:04.7 | 5:45:47 | 3:05 | 1.61 | 3 | 18 | 31.4 |
| 93 | 3:10.5 | 5:48:58 | 3:10 | 1.61 | 0 | 19 | 30.4 |
| 94 | 3:08.7 | 5:52:06 | 3:08 | 1.61 | 4 | 7 | 30.7 |
| 95 | 3:23.2 | 5:55:30 | 3:23 | 1.61 | 26 | 6 | 28.5 |
| 96 | 0:36.2 | 5:56:06 | 0:28 | 0.22 | 0 | 0 | 21.5 |

## A great week, a poor race – Butser Fell Race (27/09)

By this point in the year I had achieved some real highlights for myself, I'd almost recovered from injury which at times I'd thought would be impossible, I'd met more "real" people (not virtual ones) and enjoyed their company, I'd completed the Peak Sky race which was just a dream when I first entered, I'd completed my longest and highest ever bike ride, and I'd combined running and cycling to take part in a duathlon.

It was still only September, every race I did now I was trying to tell myself to call it quits while I was ahead, I had done more than I had planned, was getting better, but now starting to feel a little strain on my other leg, it was getting tight around the knee so I decided to start winding down my race season. This was a tough decision; I had originally decided to take part in something called the 9Bar ultra marathon which was a 50 mile race. I'd never run this distance before, I was sure I could manage it but the nagging leg was giving me concerns as to whether the time was right. Another reason for considering the race was I had a number of friends taking part, it would have been fabulous to do one last race in 2015 with friends, I'm sure they would have helped me complete it, but I took what I feel was the wise decision to not enter the race.

When I was younger, we used to do a school cross country race around Queen Elizabeth Country Park and Butser Hill. I absolutely hated this, not only was it often muddy, but it was also steep. I don't think this uncommon among runners, many seem to now love running which they hated when they were younger.

As I grew up I would notice a yearly race up and down Butser Hill either advertised in the local paper, or see it as I drove past it along the motorway or went for walks in the area. I would remember the school event and think "sod that", but then as I matured I would change that thought from a negative to a positive thought, "how amazing". I never thought I'd be fit enough to take part in this race, it's pretty tough, yet here I was, in my 40's, and getting fit enough to now consider entering.

The race is a category B fell race, just 5 miles long, about 1,200 feet (350 metres) elevation, and also has options for juniors to do shorter events. I remembered the Peak District race where I watched in awe as people far older than me (as well as younger) would hurtle down a hill without a care in the world, this was something I promised myself I'd get better at in future, so I thought this would be a great race to make a start on this promise. As a bonus I had a couple of friends also doing this race, including James Heggie who I ran with at the Chiltern race and last saw me wrapped in foil on the floor. The other guy I knew was Pete Collins, a really great runner that I'd met at Parkrun; he had also been coming back from a bad injury and was now smashing the Queen Elizabeth course in finishing times I can only dream of.

I knew the distance would not trouble me, I knew the hill well as had run up and down it many times during the year, the only variables I was unable to plan well were my legs, plus the fact I was working in Switzerland the week before. I was determined not to end the year as I did last year, working in Switzerland, arriving home late, doing a race, and injury myself, so I booked my flight home on Thursday instead of Friday. I planned no running while I was away, it was only 2 weeks between this race and my last bike race, but I stupidly still packed my running gear.

The work trip went well, long days, but very productive; however after a long day you need to do something to re-energise yourself. The hotel I stay at overlooks Lake Zurich, and is on the side of a steep hill, it's an amazing place. The evenings were getting dark, but not too cold, and were dry, so I decided on the Tuesday to just do a gentle leg stretch which ended up being 5 ½ miles, 250 metres of elevation, in around 48 minutes. I jumped straight in the hotel ice bath after, feeling fabulous.

The next night followed similar routine; I got carried away completing hill reps, 6 miles, over 400 metres of ascent, in 53 minutes. This was further and higher than the race I was due to do in just 72 hours later, I felt great after but admit it's not great race preparation.

Now I know I was stupid doing this, but when I'm away if I don't do something like this then I end up living my life working – work in the office, grab a snack from a supermarket or room service, and then work in the hotel, it not only bores the hell out of me, but also impacts my sleep and also my moods, finally impacting on my work in a negative way. With such a great location, which I don't get to see so often, I didn't want to waste my evenings doing this, or worse still sitting in the free hotel bar, drinking and feeling even worse, I had to do something productive.

When I got home, Sally took me out to treat me to a new pair of running shoes, since the Peak race where I threw away my trail shoes I had been running in just road shoes – a mixture of maximal/cushion Skechers, barefoot Merrell's, or a pair of hybrid trail/road Salomon. I picked a pair of Asics as I knew the old road shoes in this brand which I'd been using earlier in the year fitted me well. These had big lugs on these which would be great for hill running, I was going to test them on the day of the race which is never a wise decision but I had no time to break them in and figured the safety of having suitable shoes for a fell race was greater than the risk of using road shoes on a steep slope

The day of the race came, I felt okay, not great, and I was tired from the week before, I had compounded to my tiredness by doing a Parkrun the day before. I met up with James, it was really good to see him again, and we lined up together at the start line.

The start was immediately uphill, I hadn't warmed up, I was feeling tired, and my calves told me straight away that this would be tougher than I had planned.

Despite having run this hill many times during the year, my jog quickly slowed down to a hike, not a slow hike, but it was definitely a hike. James overtook me and went off ahead, I noticed he had quite a unique but obviously effective running style, but never thought about chasing him uphill.

A goal for this race was to get better at down hills, and this is where I concentrated my efforts, running more relaxed, arms out to balance myself, trying to maximise my time in the air, whilst not falling over. My legs actually felt pretty good when descending, maybe it was because I was more relaxed, the lugs on the trainers gave me much more confidence, so good in fact that I'd find myself catching and overtaking James (and many others), setting Pb's on many Strava segments. The race was 3 up hills, 3 down hills, so I thought I would maybe end up neck and neck with James at the end since he was bound to overtake me on the up hills again.

The third up hill was horrid; it was on the North side of Butser hill, not facing the sun so the grass and brambles were much denser. The track going up was rutted, narrow, and bordered a barbed wire fence. This was horrid, I had a queue of people behind me trying to get past, I was trying to keep to the left but scratching my arm on the fence and bleeding, my pace slowed down really badly, not because I was suffered for fitness or injury, it was simply because of the terrain.

I made it to the top, started to run, and then noticed my shoelace becoming loose. The trainers were fantastic, really comfortable, but I remember saying to Sally when I put them on how thin and smooth the laces were. I debated completing the run with untied shoe laces, but then realised how dangerous this could be running downhill, so I stopped, watched a James headed off into the distance, and tried to do up my shoe laces with numb Raynaud's fingers (I even had gloves on to help keep my hands warm, it worked but I had to get the gloves off with my teeth so I could do up the laces). This was again a struggle, just like the duathlon, I wish I'd got those bungee laces, but I eventually managed it and headed off to the final downhill, finishing a little after James in 46 min 30 seconds. Pete finished 2nd overall in 35m30secs, awesome result.

This time or performance wasn't great, it also wasn't bad, I had hoped for between 45 and 50 minutes, but I had also hoped to learn something about downhill running; I definitely achieved that. I think if I had been more focussed on a fast finish time, I could have pushed myself on the uphill more, I certainly would not have done hill training in Zurich the week before, and I definitely should have gone with the duathlon idea of bungee laces.

The title of this chapter says it was a great week (it was, Switzerland trip, work and running, were great, as was catching up with James), but a poor race (it was, so many schoolboy mistakes made), and I still stand by this. I know I can do better, I wasn't preparing well, still way too casual, but at least I was my competitive side was returning as a feeling, just not yet as an action.

## 5 Why's and Measures Drive Behaviours (October)

Maybe I over analyse things too much, maybe I just don't know what I want, maybe I'm never happy with what I've achieved and take continuous improvement too far, I don't know, but after recent races, plus life at work, I began to question my future quite hard. 5 Why's is a continuous improvement way of thinking to drive down to root cause, hence the title of this paragraph.

The goals for the year were complete, lots of new things to look back on (writing another book helped me reflect this rather than take things for granted), but the end goal was as unclear as ever. I had begun to enter races as I had done last year, no clear purpose.

I'm learning a lot about strategy at work this year, how you can have a vision, then produce a strategy, then a plan. Strategy usually lasts about 3 years but can be less or more, the strategy originally conceived to achieve the vision can change, and I guess that is what was happening to me as a person this year.

Last year I wanted to be the best person I could possibly be, for my wife and family, for work, and for myself. The definition of "the best person" is fluid, the best performing, the best friend, the nicest person, whatever it is, it has to be the best I can achieve. I've become far more patient over the last 12 months, more relaxed, learnt how to slow down and take time to experience things more which I think is important as this life of mine is now racing away. To say life is racing away may sound morbid, but truth is it is. This year I have 1 year less to live than I had last year, and the same will happen again tomorrow, and everyday thereafter. The opportunity to do things reduces with age, simple as that, so you need to seize the day and do things now rather than put things off.

Parkrun had helped me realise you can compete and have fun, the Southern Sportive had given me a taste of success, and I was now enjoying the smell and taste as much as one of my wife's cakes (well, almost). What I also learnt was that the current plan to achieve my goals was not working, running for pace meant running as fast as possible, it wasn't working for me at the pace I wanted, I had become better in some areas as the negative/even splits were improving, but there was still plenty of room to improve.

When I question why? I think I'm getting closer to the reason. It's definitely about bettering me, as well as experiencing new highs and lows, but deep down I think I like running for the same reason as I liked bodybuilding. I would hate a job where I go into the same office, at the same times, and sit with the same people doing the same job, every single day, which is strange as I like structure. I love my job as I never know what country, office, function, people, or topic I will be working on; but putting this uncertainty aside when I have a task I'm very structured. Bodybuilding was religiously structured; my training, food, even sleeps, was carefully planned out months in advance. With running I am not as obsessed, that's reflected in my results, but I do enjoy the structure of having a training plan to follow. I've tried just running with no plan, but for me no plan means it's very difficult to aim at a goal. Races are my goals, which is why when I've done one race I usually start planning the next one. It's a little like when you run and you're told look ahead and aim at the next landmark, run to that landmark and then start again, that's a mini plan and a mini goal. When I have no structure I feel I'm drifting aimlessly, working towards no clear goal or purpose.

As well as thinking about all this, I also thought about my behaviours. I was looking at new tech and had noticed my Garmin 220 had been replaced by a 225, the main difference with this watch was the integrated heart rate sensor. I had a heart rate strap for my 220 my rarely used it.

As a result of these two factors (pace not working so well, new tech wish list), I decided to start experimenting with heart rate running. I read up on heart rate zones, 2 for long slow runs, up to 5 for sprints, and I began.

Initially this was a pointless as running for pace, the alerts would vibrate to tell me I was too fast, and I'd ignore the alerts. With time I got better, slowing down (rarely having to worry about speeding up), but still things were not great.

I sat down and thought hard, what was I doing wrong here, why do I ignore these alerts? I decided it was partly down to a bad habit of ignoring alerts from my watch, something I had to acknowledge and break. I also realised this was partly because of my behaviours relating to seeing my pace on my watch. When I saw pace, I saw speed, and when I see speed I only see one speed which fast. I see the upper end of the pace scale as a target, for me targets are there to be beaten; it was not seen as a measure. Measures in a process are there to control things, for example an upper and a lower control limit, which keeps a process predictable and consistent, this may not mean fast but it's a reliable process (less chance of breaking down). I was now trying to make my body a predictable machine, but was still looking at the wrong measure. By this I mean I did have the right measure which was heart rate, but I also had another conflicting measure which was pace.

This is why the second part of the title chapter is "Measures drive behaviours"; I was using the wrong measures which resulted in the wrong behaviour. Using heart rate as a measure actually drives the opposite to pace in my world, I want a low heart rate to become more efficient, I have no problems aiming at the low end of my range.

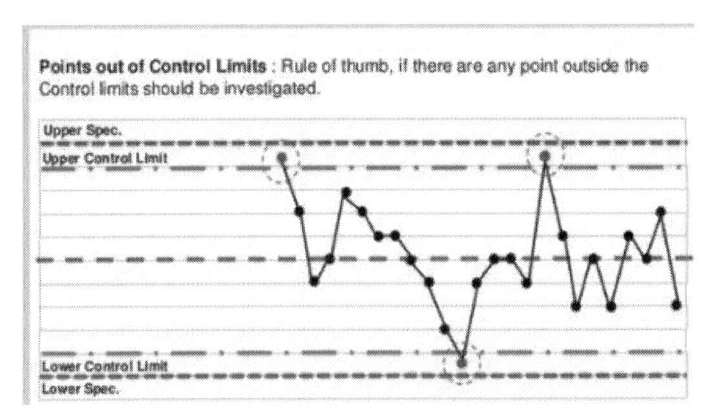


I decided to change the screen on my watch so it only showed distance, time elapsed, and heart rate, nothing else. This was quite a revelation, things improved pretty quickly, I was fairly consistent with running, much more relaxed, and my running time was not affected so much. I figured I needed to stick with this for a while to see if things improved, worst case scenario is I wouldn't be doing any worse than before as I hadn't improved that much this year, and the bonus was I was building myself a business case to invest/treat myself to the 225.

Yet again, this all linked back to my day job in which I talk about the difference of a pull versus a push process. If I concentrated on pace, for example by following a pace based training plan, then I'd be pushing my speed to perhaps an artificially high speed, eventually injuring myself. If I concentrate on hearth rate, this would eventually pull my pace upwards as I become more efficient in running, and I won't put so much risk on injuring myself.

A few weeks of practice runs and I decided to test it on a longer run, so I entered yet another race, one where I'd test the heart rate running and also incorporate a target finishing time.

## The heart rate zone, last planned race of the year – Chichester Half (11/10)

Here I am, the last race of the year, I'm writing this chapter at the end of October and still haven't entered another race for the year, I'm tempted but so far have stuck to the plan which is perfect as it gives me time to finish this book.

My heart rate test was to be the Chichester half marathon, just a 15 minute drive from my home. It was partly road/flat, and partly trail/hill. There was just one hill, but still fairly steep.

The week leading up to the race I just tapered a little, ate as normal (no carb depleting, but some extra carbs 48 hours before), and relaxed. I wanted to do well but also wanted to remember this was a heart rate test, I wanted to put the heart rate test goal before the finishing time goal.

We turned up an hour before the race, registered, and then sat in the car people watching. I hadn't done anything special for the race regarding diet, training, etc., if anything I was more laid back than ever, I hadn't even prepared my food or kit for the race until that morning. I wondered if this was going to be a race of wasted miles, I wasn't planning on it to be but the laid back preparation was telling me it was in danger of being so, I had promised in previous races to get better at this so was disappointed at this.

My plan was simple, run in heart rate zone 4 from beginning to end, and hope that my fitness was good enough to get me across the finish line in around 1hr 45m. This would be my best time for the year at this distance, but still around 15 minutes slower than 2014. It didn't matter what was going on around me, I was happy to be overtaken by whoever wanted to do this, I would not respond; I would to stick with this strategy all the way to the end. To control my heart rate better I also wanted to become more aware and controlled with my breathing. I damaged my nose when I was younger so one nostril is a little difficult to breathe through, so I tend to breath in and out through my mouth a lot, a real pain in the summer as I swallow so many bugs and flies when running, but I'd read breathing in through your nose, and out through your mouth, is beneficial. As well as this, breathing out on alternate legs is also meant to help, for example using a rhythm of 3 in, 2 out, which I'd also read helps keep your body aligned when running long distances so would help my long term leg and hip issues. This isn't as easy as it seems, I did manage it when I made myself aware of my breathing and felt very relaxed, but it was easy to slip back into old habits. I guess you can't break a habit over one short race so will continue practising.

I found out in advance the race had a few fuel stations along the way which only provided water, so learning from previous races the morning of the race I decided to take a carb drink with me, and because the Raynaud's makes it hard to hold a bottle for too long Sally bought me a handy handheld pouch holders which meant I didn't need to grip the bottle. I didn't bother with gels, jelly beans, or anything like that; the planned finish time meant I shouldn't have to worry about any further fuel.

Clothing wise I went with a short sleeved top and gloves to keep warm, shorts with calf warmers (considered long socks but I think these contributed to cramp on a recent run, too tight), and ran in a pair of newish Skechers Go-Run road trainers which I'd won on a recent Runners World "letter of the month" competition. I've been lucky in competitions this year, also won a thermal running top, a Buff, and been featured in race line photo pages. If only I'd been successful in Project 26.2 or Project Ultra, I was gutted to not be selected as I have the motivation, I just don't have the knowledge.

Ed: Hi Mark, that's a truly inspiring story. Good job on pushing through the injury lay-off and making a full recovery. Here's a pair of Skechers. Please use them responsibility – that means getting some rest days!

I don't think I could have planned the day much better than this, maybe getting this ready the day before would have been wiser. Perhaps the best way to prepare is to be laid back, not stress so much, I know I've over prepared for other races, ending up becoming so indecisive that I've ended up preparing for every eventuality, and take too much on the day?

I joined the starters in the 1h40-2h group and we edged towards the start line. Sally was stood by the side of the road with her camera ready, there was no way she was going to see me amongst all these people, so I jostled forward so she could get a good starting shot of me. As I moved myself into position I realised I had moved from my start group to the very front of the starters, great for the photo, not good for my race strategy as I knew from previous experiences I tend to get carried away with those faster runners around me.

The gun went off, I set off fast, the alerts were quickly vibrating on my wrist, and for once I listened (or felt) the alerts and slowed down.

I settled into a very steady rhythm, the alerts were still going off but I acknowledged this and slowed down, at some points I even had to speed up. Everything was going so well until we hit the trail area

My Skechers were fantastic, I've got two pairs now – one maximal/cushioning (Ultra's) which I feel like I bounce along in but suffer when running at speed, I tended to roll and injure my ankle, and the Go-Run pair which fit like a glove and are mega-light. Once I got into my "zone" I skipped along so easily, but then the trail which was peppered with stones, hard limestone, and rutted, was a little trickier to navigate. As I moved across the trails my heart rate increased, so I slowed down, then we started the gradual incline which sent the heart rate even higher. I contemplated walking to lower the rate but the sensor was telling me that I was being a lazy runner; there was some capacity to keep moving at a zone 4 pace, there was no need to use a small incline or a trail as an excuse to walk. We reached a fuel station, I didn't need to drink water but I chucked a cup over my head to cool down, and then we headed up the steepest incline to the top of a fairly high hill.

My heart rate increased a lot here, again I debated whether to stop and walk, and I didn't really know what to do as it was obvious the rate would increase as the incline increased. My legs felt fine, the hill section was quite short and would be over in less than 5 minutes, so I continued at a slow jog pace which was a challenge since this hill also had a separate time trial competition going up it – I wanted to compete on the time trial, but decided to remain focussed on the bigger goal. I'm glad I went with this decision, I got to the top feeling great, completed a circuit around the top of the hill, saw my friend Charles Rodmell taking photos and gave him a wave, then headed back downhill.

This was another dilemma, should I use my new found downhill running confidence and speed down, raising the heart rate, or should I go down slowly? I decided on the latter, I was moving out of zone 4 already anyway, I just needed to keep it as close as possible to 4 and save myself for the second half of the race.

Fall seven times, stand up eight. —Japanese proverb

This downhill was less steep than the incline and went on for quite a while, it moved from an open air grassy hill, to a forest with uneven trail underfoot. I kept glancing at my watch to see what was happening with my heart rate, it was during one of these glances that I didn't notice the ground getting particularly uneven which combined with running in road shoes made things a little tricky. Needless to say, I stumbled; well it wasn't a stumble, more a tumble. I hit the ground hard, one arm struggling to limit the impact as it had my bottle strapped to it, so I fell to one side and then onto my back, my bottle flying across the path of other runners who were stopping to ask if I were ok. A little embarrassed, very bruised, and as I'd find out later, quite cut up, I told them I was fine, saying "I always fall over in races" (which is pretty close to the truth), then dusted myself off and continued running.

I had wrapped my tight knee up with some KT tape before the race, the fall had made it come lose, over the next mile or so it because really lose and began flapping around, so I ripped off the remaining sections which was a shame as I felt like it had been helping. I'm not really sure how sticking tape on my leg helps, maybe it's just placebo effect, but given the issues I had this year I'm happy to try anything out of sheer desperation. Luckily I knew the rest of the race was fairly flat so there was less pressure on my sore legs from there to the finish line.

I visit Chichester a lot, loads of good restaurants there, plus I cycle the area all the time through the South Downs, but the race took me to routes I've never been to, I was running in a familiar area but an unfamiliar route, so despite me being able to count down the miles, and work out we were heading back to the start/finish line, I had no idea what was ahead – road, trail, etc. What I did know was there would be no more elevation of note, so I relaxed into my zone 4 pace and started working out in my head if I'd be finishing in my 1 hr 45 m finishing goal time.

Do you ever do maths in your head when running? I love to do this, on a treadmill it relieves the boredom, out of the road it's a little trickier as I get distracted by other things around me, on this run it was quite a challenge as I didn't have any data fields showing current race or lap pace, so I started working backwards from time elapsed divided by distance run, giving me a pace, and then used that pace to project forwards to expected finishing time. I was well happy; with 3 miles to go I realised I was well on track to beat my goal without evening focussing on it. I knew that with these calculations I'd included slower pace at the hill so all things being well it would be even better than I'd calculated.

As I ran the last few miles yet another person came running up behind me asking if I'd fallen over. I had no idea at this point that I was covered in a mixture of mud and blood on the back on my leg, arm and shoulder, but I was happy to admit to this woman that I had, there was no point in denying the obvious. I am terrible with names of strangers so I didn't ask her name, I remember she said she had won the Chichester half a year or so ago, had recently had a baby boy, and was now getting back into running. We ran together for much of the rest of the race, not sure if I slowed her down or not but she seemed happy enough to chat. As we approached a mile to go she said she was going to see how she felt and kick on, I was determined to stick to my zone 4 plan so wished her all the best and off she went. I'm glad I met this lady, firstly she was obviously a far better than runner than me but was kind enough to keep me company for a while, and secondly to hear her story about winning before, having a baby, and now making a comeback was really inspiring for me.

Now usually in the final miles of a race I'm hanging in there having set off too fast, not taken on enough fuel, or injured. This race was really, really different.

We got to the end of what I think was a disused railway line, and was about to take a turn left onto a road I knew well, I cycled along it all the time. Knowing I wasn't about to make the same mistake as in the 100 mile bike race and that it was just a short sprint to the end, I decided to ignore my heart rate monitor and kick for home. I was both amazed and also a little ashamed, I had so much power left in my legs, and my pace quickened from the regular 5 min/km pace of the previous 20km, to something closer to 4 min/km for the final 1.1km, my heart rate only rose from around 160 to 170 beats per minute. I was ashamed as I overtook several people in this final sprint, people who had been in front of me for 20km and then there I was, nipping in and stealing their places at the end, I hated doing that, felt so unsporting, but also great – I guess my competitive streak was well and truly starting to return.

I finished the race in 1 hour 42 minutes, 39 seconds, placing 90th out of 734. I finished sprinting, uninjured, no cramps, and feeling fresh, a bonus was an amazing goodie bag containing Montezuma chocolate and Bodyshop treats. I looked around for Charles at the end, his wife was also running the race, but despite doing laps looking for him I never found him, that was a shame as would have been great to chat but food was calling so off Sally and I went for pizza and cake.

So this was my last race of the year, I can award this the title of "Best performance of the year"; I have never felt as happy with my performance as I had done here.

I don't think there was much I would change from this race, based on results I was incredibly happy. The dilemma when running up and down hill with heart rate was something to challenge in the future, but apart from that it would be just about becoming fitter as measured by heart rate, and hoping increased pace would be pulled through.

## Holiday, I need a break

Just as we'd done in June for Sally's birthday, we took time off in October for my birthday.

Last year, as a special treat for my birthday, I decided I wanted to stay at home and run my first Ultra marathon, the Stort30. This year, having had quite a stressful time physically and mentally, in and out of work, and to try sticking to my rule of no more races, I decided to book a lazy holiday to Crete for a week. The plan was to simply do nothing, maybe a tiny bit of running, but mostly (weather permitting) to laze around the pool, eat and drink whatever I wanted, and just recharge.

We stayed at a beautiful hotel, Mitsis Laguna; well it was beautiful on the surface at least. Maybe expectations change through experience, maybe it's attention to detail, perhaps it's the sign of a busy hotel coming to the end of a long hard season, or maybe it was just me with my continuous improvement hat on, but scrub a little under the surface and there were definite areas for improvement.

I stuck to the plan of minimal running, just 4 runs and 30km in total over the 7 days, I reckon Sally and I walked twice that distance together. I swam a lot, getting better and better at front crawl while enjoying kicking my legs especially hard and splashing the kids and adults who would just annoy me floating around all day on inflatables in the pool.

I read lots as well on holiday, some were work related but more about the mind, how it works which made my mind work harder and ponder what next for me, Sally, and our future.

While laying on my sun lounger, reading and thinking, I'd look into the distance and see mountains inland, they looked tempting, I debated hiring a car to go hiking, but time went so quick (strange how time can go so quick despite me doing nothing) and before I knew it we were due to go home. Maybe another year we can go back and do some hiking, I know Sally is afraid of heights so it may be a loose definition of mountain hiking, but the countryside and mountains looked great.

We headed home on the Friday, back to work Monday, and life quickly settled into our routine. I do like routine, the more I think about it perhaps this is why I enjoy running as it gives me structure and routine.

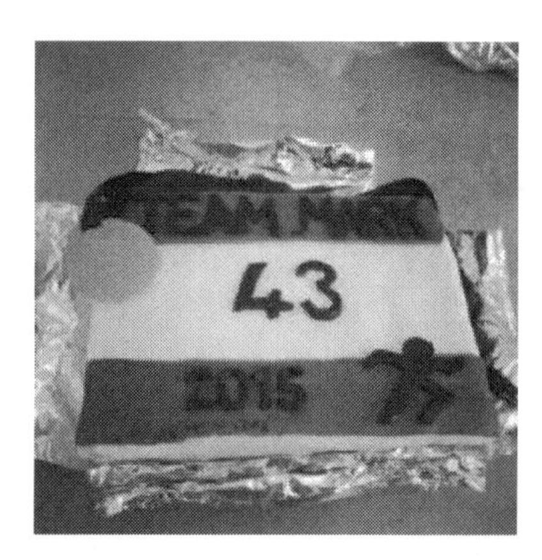


To some this may appear a pointless chapter to some as it's got very little to do with running but to me it's got plenty to do with running and links back to the bodybuilding days when I found it difficult to switch off and wind down, or even the same time last year when holiday was about running an ultra-marathon during a period when I was injured. This year I listened to my body, I took a break, and spent quality time with Sally. Despite it being my birthday, I always say to her that the best present I could have is for her to relax and enjoy herself, she makes sure every day of the year feels like it's my birthday.

Sally also made my birthday special by baking me a birthday cake, I ate half before holiday and the other half straight after, and it was fantastic. Doesn't matter how much money you have, you can't buy a homemade cake, this is always my favourite birthday and Christmas present – thank you Sally x.

## What next?

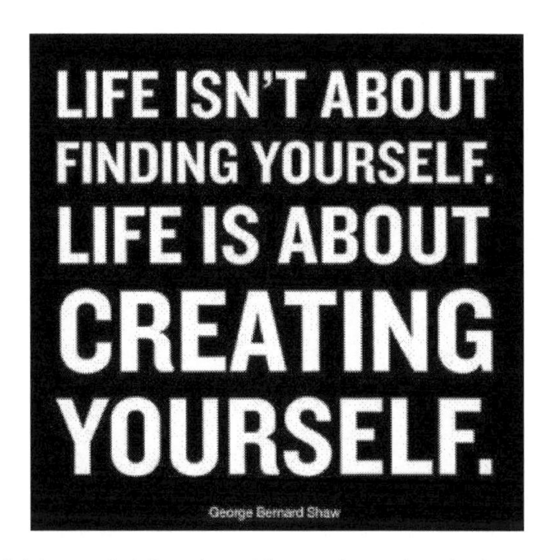


I thought about lots of things on holiday; about life in and out of work, about where my future was heading, and a little about running. I had already started writing this book before the holiday so was thinking about completing it, what I'd done so far in the year, what was left to do (mostly work related), and what my goals were (maybe more non work related).

I had started running in 2013, I had started taking dipping my toes in participating in races in 2014, and then this year I had enjoyed taking this another level by go further, higher, meeting more people, visiting new places and taking part in new disciplines. As the year was coming to an end I began to regain my appetite for competing against others, to experience the thrill of overtaking people and running faster. I got frustrated at this, I had the urge but didn't have the tools, physically I hadn't trained for speed, and mentally I wasn't ready. Don't get me wrong, I like being a nicer person, it's far better than being aggressive with people whether it is verbally or physically, but nothing beats the thrill of pushing me not only against my own limits but also against others.

I decided on the following plan for 2016 to try to do something about this,

1. First quarter of the year, go back to basics, get a speed base and build up to a fast half marathon in February, it would be great to beat my personal best of 1h33m. This would be the start of my competitive stage. I've entered the Worthing Half Marathon for this
2. Middle of the year to race abroad I will focus on another goal of mine, back to the "experiencing new things goal" and race abroad. I will combine this with our June holiday, ideally an ultra-marathon but if shorter then fine, so long as it's in an awesome place. I'm looking at a Skyrace in Madeira in June which will combine my hobby of running with Sally's of horticulture, bit of a problem with dates and holidays though so I may have to find a plan B
3. Third quarter of the year, I will run a new experience race in the UK. I've entered the Snowdonia Trail Marathon, run by Always Aim High, on 24$^{th}$ July for this. Mount Snowdon is the UK's 2$^{nd}$ highest peak, just under 1,100 metres

4. Final quarter of the year, back to racing, I would love to set a personal best in the 10 mile which would be 71 minutes. I'd also like to take part in one of these larger, more commercial events which I say I hate the thought of but never entered. I need to do this to see if what I think is actually true, I think I'd hate it, but I've never done such an event, feelings need to be turned into facts, or maybe I'll enjoy it? This will probably be the Great South Run in October. It fills me with dread thinking about it, my continuous improvement/Lean thinking head is busy thinking about the difference between cycle and lead time, value add and non-value add time. By this I mean the race will take around 75 minutes (value add/cycle time), but because of the massive organisation of the event I'm likely to have to turn up early, wait around, and then race, so total time (lead time) for the event will probably be closer to 3 ½ hours
5. Over the year I will also go regularly sub 20 in Parkrun, maybe do some in new locations and meet up with friends

And how will I do this

1. Physical: I will try to stay injury free over the winter, train only for short distance races, intervals and hill reps, run no further than half marathon, this also means I can use the treadmill if needed
2. Technique: I've been analysing my running this year a lot, as well as linking to cause and effect which is something I talk about a lot at work. When you run you have several key factors. You have pace which is the effect and you cadence and stride length which are the causes. It's then a simple calculation of (cadence x stride length) / distance which give your finishing time. I've looked at these causes, compared to other runners I know, and looked for my weak point which is stride length; my cadence is almost always above 180 which is really good. So I will look at ways to increase stride length which will be through increasing flexibility in my hips, glutes and legs, and not by over-reaching
3. Specialise: I will concentrate on competing just in running, nothing else. For cross training I may take part in bike events or duathlons
4. Diet: A neglected part of my 2015 plan, get down to a race weight of 80kg, I'm currently 88kg, as I feel this will give me the biggest gain. In bodybuilding it was always 75% is about diet, I need to listen to my advice, it worked so well in the past, I've just got greedy lately as running for fun meant there was no pressure to diet

I will try harder than ever before, I may not achieve my goals but at least I've set them and also have a plan, that's the first step. I know how my mind works, set a goal and then do whatever it takes to get as close as possible to it, but will not make the same mistakes as in bodybuilding, I will be mindful of others around you.

I also think by setting these goals and changing my mind-set and behaviour, I will change at work. I have always said I want to have the choice to retire at 50, I may decide not to do this, but I think my wind down to retirement has maybe started a little too early as I still have 7 years to go, so I hope this will keep my pushing myself a little longer.

When I started my current job I was still competitive in bodybuilding, as I mentioned before I can't pretend to be two people, it's all or nothing, and the competitive streak made me a total arse of a manager, I was trying to go fast but going alone, I need to run with my team. I quit the bodybuilding to fix that, toughest and hardest decision of my life, but one which was for the best.

This was me in one of my first shows, happy on the outside, lonely on the inside

And this was my last show, one of the saddest days of my life; lonely and sad on the outside, on reflection maybe the start of becoming one of the happiest on the inside

I won't go into plans for work, these are not really known, I still enjoy working for my current employer, it's a bit of a cliché but it's the people I work with (including my boss) who make it so enjoyable. I do know that I feel the urge to do something different, maybe more vocational, more often than I used to.

I love this Steve Jobs quote, I follow it every day. Even writing this book, which was a lot of work, seemed easy as I loved what I was writing about and I loved the thought of people hopefully enjoying reading it.

My values have changed, running with and meeting some fabulous people who are less driven by careers, wealth, and other material things, makes me ponder "what do I need vs what do I want?" There's a noticeable difference between the answers to both questions, I have started to simplify my life by taking away some of the things I don't need and it feels great. I need to feel that what I do adds value in some way, not just to me but to others around me.

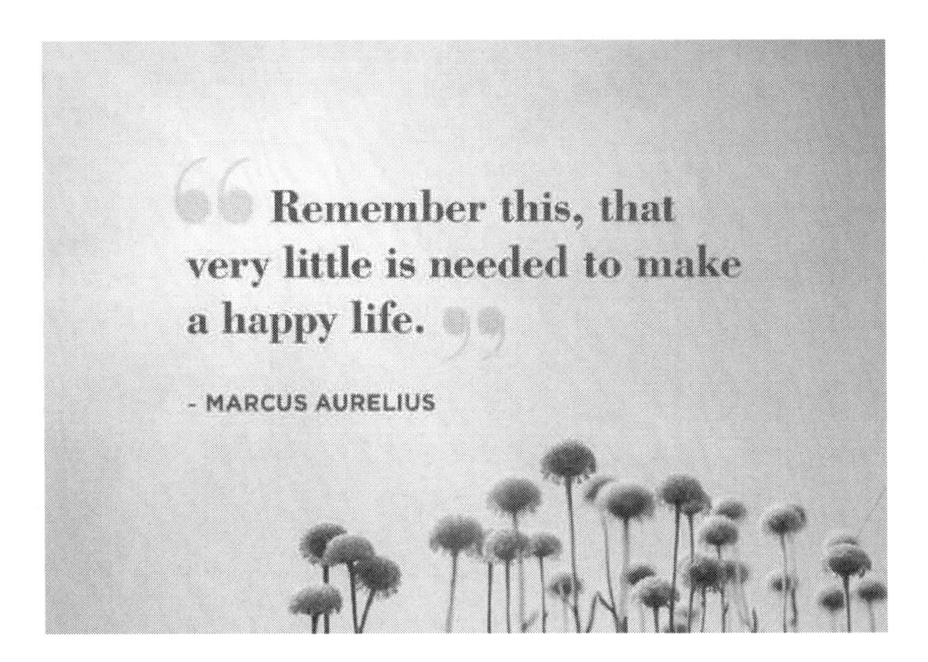


Long term I have a vision of my future, it's always in my head; I also have photographs of places like this to inspire me. It involves a small home in a warm country to help with my Raynaud's, with land for Sally to grow flowers and vegetables, trees with fruits on, a balcony/terrace from our bedroom, close to the sea but in a village in the country, hopefully near some hills. We will both still work, Sally will be doing something linked to baking or growing, I will do something involving the outdoors, both will be more about giving back to others. We will also be integrated into the local village community, I remember when I was young visiting my nan, doors were always open for visitors, the old men sat on chairs outside chatting, that's what I want. This is it so far, a simple but fulfilling life, where we will live together in a happy and simple life. Here are a few of my vision photos, the fruit tree, the balcony, and the woman.

## Training

A review of my first book mentioned the lack of insights into my training, so I thought rather than give a blow by blow account of my training leading up to every race I did this year I'd wrap it up into one chapter. Advance warning, it won't be a long chapter, I have no right to coach people on training as I've lost every race, I'm poor at training. I have tried to get onto the Runners World Project 26.2 and also Project Trail teams so I could learn, but not yet been accepted, I try again in 2016. What I can do is motivate and inspire people to train, compete, or just try something new.

At the beginning of the year I was injured, I was desperate, and I hadn't managed any exercise of note for weeks, but I had the 3 Forts Challenge coming up so had to find an intensive marathon training plan. I searched Google and settled on something which the words "advanced", "marathon", and "training plan" in it.

I couldn't walk let alone run at this point, so I took the plan, got on my road bike and followed the plan. The plan was based on distance, so for the bike I simply doubled the distances, that was it. There were no interval or hill sessions in this plan, I did that on purpose as I knew speed was not going to be possible, and for the hills I would just be walking them slowly. As my leg got better I did get on the stepper and stair climber in the gym to get my body in better shape for the hill hiking in the race.

With about a month to go before the race I felt confident enough to do some of the runs in the plan on my feet, not the long weekend run but just the short runs of up to 10 miles or so. I stupidly ended up pushing these runs a little further, no doubt not helping me leg and annoying my physio (who I am still seeing even now, in October, almost a year after the injury), but if I couldn't walk a reasonable distance then there was no point lining up on the start line – they was no option to complete the race on a mountain bike.

By the middle of the year, when the 3 Forts was finished I continued with the same plan, but ran more on my legs, going further and including some hills on the runs. I decided to add in more hills then in the plan as I knew the elevation in the races to come later in the year would get tougher. The Trionium and Chiltern races could also be classed as my training, everything has to have a purpose in my life, and these races had a purpose on my end goal, the Peak Sky race. They not only prepared me for distance and elevation, but also for nutrition plus running with people. This last item is underestimated; running with others can be enjoyable but also can totally ruin race plans. You can get carried away with pace running in a group, you can talk too much and waste oxygen, you will find running in large crowds frustrating as you can only move at the pace of the slowest moving person.

As I worked through this period, I realised I was feeling knackered, I was so tired all the time and getting a little moody at home. I acknowledged the reason for this was the training plan, doing it on a bike was fine, I'm a pretty good cyclist, but on my feet was tough. I'm an average runner, but hadn't run far for a long time; my training plan was an advanced plan, far too advanced for me.

I found a more suitable plan for my level, more short runs, better structured hill repeats, plus the odd interval session. I still also included long cycle rides at the weekend to keep the distances up. For me distance is as much a mental as it is a physical challenge – get over the words 50 or 100 km/miles in your head, then the physical side feels so much easier. This plan also involved 3 weeks of tapering which was ideal for the Peak race, 3 weeks between Chiltern and Peak races meant I just relaxed and concentrated on the diet side of things.

The second half of the year I started using the Asics plan. This was really useful, very adaptable, you just pick the race distance, number of weeks to train, effort level, number of runs per week, plus there's the ability to change it as you go along. This is all I followed, as well as continuing to go to the gym for one or two strength sessions a week plus the odd bike ride (which have reduced a lot due to shorter, wetter and colder days). It was during this period I started feeling better mentally about racing, when the competitive urge started to return.

As one of my chapters mentioned, I finally decided to change focus from pace to heart rate, which is where I am now at, still very early stages. I stuck with the Asics app for a while, if it was a slow pace run I use heart rate zone 2 or 3, if it's a fast run I go zone 5, and threshold is usually around 4(ish). I've now switched to a half marathon schedule for the winter, no need for long runs over the winter, and decided to switch to one of the Garmin half marathon training plans which use only heart rate, there is no mention at all about pace. This follows the theory I had about paying no attention at all to pace, letting your heart rate pull your fitness up which in turn will pull your pace up, as opposed to pushing pace on your body by following a pace plan.

Now I've started using heart rate better I also decided to update my Garmin 220 to a 225, no more need for a strap strap. I was in a dilemma over this, 10 hrs battery life is not enough to last a 50 mile race, should I go with a Fenix and stick with chest strap, go with another brand of watch, or just lower my goals. I went with lowering my goals, no way with work could I find the time to train and compete in a 50 mile race. I'm a little disappointed about this, as soon as I upgraded I noticed Garmin announced the 235, a longer battery life, integrated heart rate sensor, basically everything I wanted in my dilemma all in one neat watch. What I've also found is with the poor circulation in my hands, the wrist based heart rate is pretty erratic, I can be sprinting and the heart rate drops to sub 100. It helps if I wear long sleeves, gloves, wear the watch higher up my arm (but then you can't see it as you've got long sleeves), so I've also bought one of the new heart rate chest straps.

I was in a taxi coming back from working in Switzerland and was boring my taxi driver with my stories, I was talking a lot on this pull/push theory (linked really closely to my day job), and also upper and lower control points. As he drives all day, he understood the pace equals speed equals fast theory in my book. I asked him if he thought roads would flow smoother and less accidents would happen if we introduced lower as well as upper control limits to our roads, just like we do in processes and I was now trying to do in my running. He agreed, the lack of a lower limit does not help, and acknowledged the upper limit is just a target for him; he will always edge past the limit.

So that's my training summarised, I'm not going to publish pages on training plans, it's pointless, everyone is different. It used to, and still does, make me laugh when I was bodybuilding, where you'd see people in the gym with the latest magazine, trying to follow a plan which someone has themselves just copy and pasted. These plans are not personal to you, only you know your body, you can tell if you feel injured, tired, faster, slower, losing weight, gaining weight, happy or unhappy – just search the net, find something to base your training on, and then educate yourself and learn from experience. The Asics plan is probably the most adaptable of all those I've found, I don't think you can go wrong starting with this, but for the end of 2015 and early 2016 I'm switching to the heart rate half marathon training plan simply because I want to really give this method of training my best shot, plus it involves more speed and hill work. If I used the Asics site it would be back to running with pace goals which for me is not a wise move, as I said in the previous chapter, I want to stay injury free as much as possible, I've proved to myself pace does not help here.

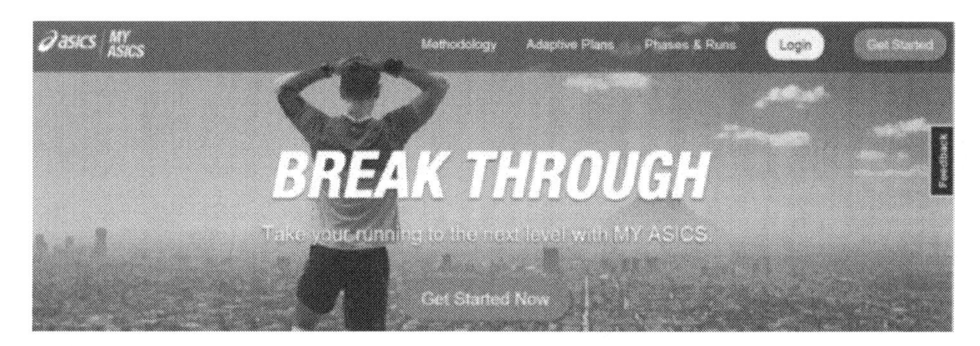

## Diet

So here's another short chapter for you, in response to feedback on the last book. To save a few moments of your valuable time, if you're happy with your body weight or size then probably no need to read this, skip onto the next chapter, I don't want people reading this and then complaining it was rubbish or worse still, put doubts in their minds about whether they truly are happy with their diet.

Bottom line here is I've gained weight in 2015, probably around 5kg, so I can't give you diet advice. I know what I should do, but I don't listen to my own advice. I know I should split have the biggest meal of the day in the morning, and then the calories per meal throughout the rest of the day should gradually decrease, as should the volume of carbs which are replaced with fibrous veg, salad, or even fats. This means I would be consuming less calories at the end of the day, which makes sense as that's when I'm usually sat at home needing no fuel for my body or brain.

This was so easy to do when bodybuilding, I had no choice as I didn't want to look like an overweight idiot on stage in a tiny pair of sparkly pants with glitter tan all over me showing off my imperfections. I was competing back then, there was a reason to diet hard, be a little miserable, but to look awesome (in the judge's eyes). This was my second show, the British Nationals, where I came 3rd in my class – I still saw my imperfections in the mirror, focussed on the fat that was left, not the fat I'd lost.

Over the last two years of running I've not competed, I've taken part, my weight has fluctuated but no by so much, I've not had to buy larger clothes, so why starve myself of food that I enjoy?

I admit I've become complacent with the diet, skipping breakfast quite often, eating poorly while working away, having sneaky spoons of peanut butter and Nutella straight for the jar in the evening, and enjoying many other nice treats like Sally's cakes.

The best bit of diet advice I can give is firstly find a good reason to diet. If it's to compete then as I say, you have no choice but to look after the diet. If's it to look or feel good then take a look at yourself in the mirror (maybe you need to do this naked); if you see yourself as fat and unhappy then keep looking in that mirror every day whilst also imagining the food you ate over the previous 24 hours and the exercise you didn't do. You can probably see a reflection of the food you ate or the lack of exercise in the mirror. The formula is simple, eat badly + move little = look and feel that way. May sound harsh, but that's what I do myself, I hate the sight I see in the mirror some days, I don't ignore it though, sometimes I even take a photo and post online, not because I'm proud but because I'm ashamed and need to shame myself into doing something about it. The reflection you see in the mirror can only be seen through your eyes, even in the photo above I'd look at myself in the mirror and see myself as fat at the time, bodybuilders are probably the worst when it comes to eating disorders but not seeing it for themselves, that's why they're always seeking reassurance from others.

So use the pyramid theory, start big and end the day smaller. If you feel hunger pangs, these are either a cause of you adapting your diet in the early stages (so stick with it), boredom (so find something interesting to do), and genuine hunger (go fill up on good stuff, veg, salad, fruit, or try eating your food slower). When bodybuilding I found a neat trick was to eat my smaller meals with smaller knives and forks, so I couldn't shovel the food down my neck so quick. There's also the idea of using smaller plates so you eat less.

As I said at the start, I'm no dietician, like the training you should be able to learn what to eat and when. I doubt a kid is reading this section so we're all adults and know what is good and bad. If you chose to ignore your mirror image, your life experience and even those annoying programmes on TV, then I can't see how a total stranger like me or someone else can convince you otherwise.

This year I've eaten loads of beetroot, I've been peeing red most of the year thanks to it growing so well on the allotment. I've had it in soup, in coleslaw, pickled, hoummus, raw, even in cake. It's meant to help with nitric oxide I think, I don't know if it works, I just know it tastes great, so I eat it.

I've also experimented with chia seeds; again I don't know the science behind these but was recommended them by others as meant to give you energy. They are a seed just like pumpkin seeds, so they contain healthy fats, but I'm not sure how they are better than pumpkin or any other seeds. I buy them online as they cost a lot on the high street, I've used them in my porridge and smoothies, if you leave them overnight in liquid they swell up and some say it looks like frog spawn. I don't know if they have helped me recover or run longer, they certainly haven't helped me get faster, but they've not harmed me and when you're as desperate as I was earlier in the year you'll try anything so I will continue with them over the winter.

Regarding supplements, if I'm feeling lazy and find some protein powder on offer I may buy the odd tub but I've preferred real food this year, I don't need to volume of protein as a bodybuilder needs. I have taken a few pre-workout supplements, these are always good for a buzz before exercise, I can definitely feel the difference, problem is I usually also drink strong coffee and overdose on caffeine which gives me a dodgy stomach or leads to dehydration. Charles Rodmell sent me something called Argi+ which is L-Arginine, it's meant to help with the flow of red blood cells, and he thought it may help with my Raynaud's. I think it did a little, can't say for sure as only took a couple of small sachets, I also wore gloves on those days and maybe the weather was better, so I've now bought something similar from a health food shop to help me through the winter. That's about it for supplements, I was rattling like a chemists bag when bodybuilding, try to keep things simpler now I'm running.

My best pre-race fuel has varied depending on the type of race. For shorter races (say 1 ½ hours long) I've just had tinned fruit, including the syrup, which gives me a quick hit of energy, this is important since on a short race you don't really want to be stopping for or carrying food with you. The handheld bottle I used on the Chichester race was great as a backup, I didn't waste energy gripping it and just swigged from it as I needed, no playing around with gels which often burst in my pocket or worse still, the Raynaud's means I can't even hold them.

For the longer races I've not worked out what is best, rice pudding is great, oats have been okay, bagels with peanut butter and jam have worked fine, but to be honest I don't think it really matters as long as you have fuel in you. On the long races you can tap into the food stored in your body which you've built up in the days leading up to the race, you've not been exercising so much so it's not gone anywhere, plus there's the bonus of fat it can tap into if it really needs it. I think for long runs it's more important to plan what to eat or drink during the race, have quick release food on a regular basis, carb drinks on the go, and water (plenty of) to drink or simply chuck over you to rehydrate. I haven't really used gels during the year, preferred things like shot blocks, jelly sweets or just making use of fuel stations better. I've taken 3 gels with me on many of the longer races and they always are there at the end. I've had the same 3 since last year; they have an expiry date of May 2015 and will probably still be carried next year "just in case". Worst thing to do would be use them because I have them, on top of the other food on offer in races, and take on too much food, I'm not as greedy as I used to be.

One closing item on this topic, my wife does not eat meat, but she does eat fish (she's a pescatarian. I do find myself losing weight, toning up, and feeling better when I cut back on meat and eat more like her, she's slim and maintains her weight really easy. During the week I probably only eat meat 3 times a week now, so different to when I used to eat around a 1kg of chicken or turkey every day when bodybuilding. In 2016 I will tidy up my diet more so I can compete, the easiest way I will do this is to continue reducing meat consumption, not because I'm anti meat eaters, I love a good steak, but it just seems to work for me and my diet. Also remember that not all meat is built the same, a fist sized portion of chicken will have less calories than the same size of lamb, and if you move onto the same sized portion of processed or formed meat (grill steak, burger, etc.), then it gets worse. If what you are currently doing isn't working then why not try reducing meat, replace with fish or vegetarian alternatives, they are at least just as nice, even nicer if you ask me.

I'm not saying any of the above will work for everyone, I've met many great runners who seem to be able to eat whatever they like and not put on weight, but it works for me. I'm also realising that long slow runs in heart rate zone 2 will also help loads, I used to long slow runs but they were not much slower than my fast runs, now I'm learning better and my body shape is changing quite quick.

## Wrap Up

That's it; I've come to the final chapter, the final chapter for this year at least, looking back on the year I think it's been pretty good. I've been inspired by others books and tales, some really great adventures which I'm either not able to afford or which are maybe beyond me, but I didn't make excuses and decided to live my own adventures instead. I hope this helps do the same to you, be inspired by others but remember you don't have to follow in their steps; you can create your own path instead.

I published my first book in February, after I injured myself in December, thankfully this year (up to November) I have finished in a better physical and mental shape. I still some niggles which mostly involves a tight left knee but then at 43 years old I'm going to have to get used to.

To sum up, this year has been about going further than before with others, next year I'm going to try balancing this off with also going faster but alone. I don't know how I will manage this, I'm usually an all or nothing kind of person, but I'm hoping with my friends, work colleagues, and my own self-awareness, I will notice if I way too much back to the dark side. If I go into a silent mode for a short period then it's because I like my own thinking time, but if I turn into a self-obsessed idiot again feel free to tell me.

Looking at the word and page count for the draft of the book, this year has been more interesting than last year despite it being a shorter race season, at least that's what I'm hoping anyway. For me it's been great, a year of firsts, a year of continuous improvement, proving to myself that despite an ageing body I can do better than I did before. I have been inspired by others, I may not have done the amazing things I've seen them do, but at least I've pushed my own boundaries further than before. We may not have the capabilities, opportunities, money, or time, to do what others do, but there's no need to be jealous, go create your own personal adventures instead. I really hope I continue to do this at home and at work in 2016.

I do hope a longer book doesn't mean less interesting or boredom for those reading it, if it did then I'm really sorry. If you liked this book please do me one small favour, please rate this book on Amazon, it takes seconds to do. Having 4,000 people download it is great, but only 1% of those who downloaded the first book rated it which for me means I have no idea what 3,960 thought of it and that's not good when you're trying to write a second book, customer feedback is so important.

**If you have enjoyed this book then I would really, really, appreciate you rating this on Amazon. Their system asks you to do this after the last page is read; it takes seconds to do and would mean a lot to me. I see far too often around me how little the words "thank you" are used, just 2 words, 8 letters, but mean so much to so many.**

Thank you for reading right to the end, special thanks to the woman on the next few pages x

Sally was brave enough to climb Mount Sinai in Egypt with me, she hates heights and we weren't dressed for mountain climbing

After my second bodybuilding show, the British Nationals, where I came 3rd on my class

Our wedding day in Malta

This picture was at a party held by Estee Lauder where Sally works; she was celebrating 25 years working for them

## Appendix

### 2015 Race History

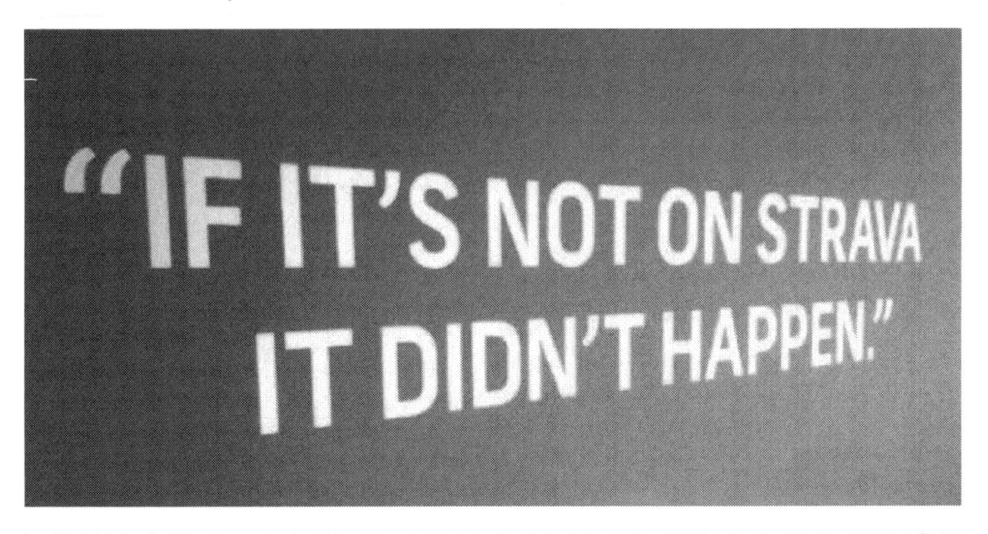

10:00 AM on Sunday, May 3, 2015

**Three forts challenge**

Under prepared, cramps, poor shoes, hit goal for sub 5 and no injury

| 43.7 km | 4:57:16 | 6:48 /km |
|---|---|---|
| Distance | Elapsed Time | Pace |

| | | | |
|---|---|---|---|
| Elevation | 947m | Calories | 4,439 |
| Moving Time | 4:54:13 | | |

Device: Garmin Forerunner 220 — Shoes: Kammor trail shoes (449.3 km)

9:11 AM on Sunday, May 17, 2015

**Sam's ride and a bit**

Got lost, extra 6 miles

3   

STRAVA LABS
View Flybys ›

| 90.4 km | 3:04:01 | 580 m |
|---|---|---|
| Distance | Moving Time | Elevation |

| 169 W | 1,862 kJ |
|---|---|
| Estimated Avg Power | Energy Output |

| | Avg | Max |
|---|---|---|
| Speed | 29.5km/h | 51.1km/h |
| Cadence | 57 | 120 |
| Calories | 2,076 | |
| Elapsed Time | 3:07:08 | |

Device: Garmin Forerunner 220 — Bike: road bike

9:05 AM on Sunday, June 14, 2015

**Trionium munro**

.044 k climb/km

| 21.2 km | 2:22:31 | 6:43 /km |
|---|---|---|
| Distance | Elapsed Time | Pace |

| | | | |
|---|---|---|---|
| Elevation | 923m | Calories | 2,324 |
| Moving Time | 2:20:21 | | |

Device: Garmin Forerunner 220 — Shoes: ASICS New black/green trail shoes (56.8 km)

8:04 AM on Sunday, June 28, 2015

## Portsmouth Change Gear 60 mile sportive on bald tyres !

my longest and highest ride to date, the day after returning from a 10 days all inclusive holiday i'm happy with that

STRAVA LABS
View Flybys ›

| 91.1km | 3:16:31 | 1,020m |
|---|---|---|
| Distance | Moving Time | Elevation (?) |

| 167W | 1,973kJ |
|---|---|
| Estimated Avg Power | Energy Output |

| | Avg | Max |
|---|---|---|
| Speed | 27.8km/h | 59.4km/h |
| Calories | 2,200 | |
| Temperature | 19°C | |
| Elapsed Time | 3:17:38 | |

Device: Garmin Edge 500 Bike: road bike

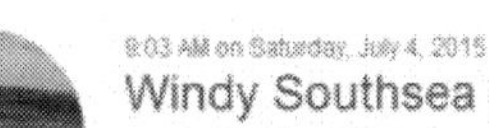

9:03 AM on Saturday, July 4, 2015

## Windy Southsea parkrun in new trainers

24/239, 3rd in age group

| 5.0km | 21:37 | 4:18/km |
|---|---|---|
| Distance | Elapsed Time | Pace |

| | | | |
|---|---|---|---|
| Elevation | 0m | Calories | 505 |
| Moving Time | 21:37 | | |

Device: Garmin Forerunner 220 Shoes: Brooks No idea My flamingo pink shoes (67.0 km)

10:03 AM on Sunday, July 5, 2015

## Summer plod in new trainers

Too much tarmac for shoe choice , big blisters

| 34.0km | 3:25:04 | 6:01/km |
|---|---|---|
| Distance | Elapsed Time | Pace |

| | | | |
|---|---|---|---|
| Elevation | 720m | Calories | 3,476 |
| Moving Time | 3:22:01 | | |

Device: Garmin Forerunner 220 Shoes: Kammer trail shoes (449.3 km)

9:04 AM on Saturday, July 11, 2015

## Xnrg Chiltern ultra race

20 mile onwards rubbush, got lost, cramps, sore leg, a litre of liquid drank, then passed out at the end - completed it

...

| 51.0km | 6:03:04 | 7:07/km |
|---|---|---|
| Distance | Elapsed Time | Pace |

| | | | |
|---|---|---|---|
| Elevation | 797m | Calories | 5,171 |
| Moving Time | 6:02:01 | | |

Device: Garmin Forerunner 220 Shoes: ASICS (884.1 km)

8:59 AM on Saturday, July 18, 2015

## Southsea parkrun, 19th out of 231

Add a description

| 5.0km | 20:23 | 4:03/km |
|---|---|---|
| Distance | Elapsed Time | Pace |

| | | | |
|---|---|---|---|
| Elevation | 0m | Calories | 501 |
| Moving Time | 20:23 | | |

Device: Garmin Forerunner 220 Shoes: Brooks No idea My flamingo pink shoes (67.0 km)

9:01 AM on Saturday, July 25, 2015

Week 2 of 3 taper, Southsea parkrun in old trainers (500 miles), 15th overall, 1st in age category

Add a description

5.0km 20:39 4:07/km
Distance Moving Time Pace

Elevation 0m Calories 501
Elapsed Time 20:39

Device: Garmin Forerunner 220 Shoes: ASICS (884.1 km)

8:08 AM on Sunday, August 2, 2015

Peak Skyrace, much slower than I wanted but met some lovely people,saw awesome places, and finished pretty fresh

Biggest learning point, shoes ! Insoles slipped out halfway round then shoe split on side - only second race in them

48.3km 6:57:14 8:37/km
Distance Elapsed Time Pace

Elevation 1,573m Calories 5,117
Moving Time 6:34:33

Device: Garmin Forerunner 220 Shoes: Kalenji green trail ones (178.3 km)

9:02 AM on Saturday, August 8, 2015

Southsea parkrun, not feeling it today, legs heavy, massive breakfast, nice swim though & treated myself to more trainers

Cadence 183 stride 1.31m 26th/278 2nd in age group

5.0km 20:49 4:09/km
Distance Moving Time Pace

Elevation 0m Calories 502
Elapsed Time 20:49

Device: Garmin Forerunner 220 Shoes: Brooks No idea My flamingo pink shoes (67.0 km)

9:02 AM on Saturday, August 15, 2015

Another ace positive split Southsea parkrun, best time this year

Add a description

5.0km 20:17 4:03/km
Distance Moving Time Pace

Elevation 0m Calories 501
Elapsed Time 20:17

Device: Garmin Forerunner 220 Shoes: Brooks No idea My flamingo pink shoes (67.0 km)

9:03 AM on Saturday, August 22, 2015

Southsea parkrun another poor positive split

Add a description

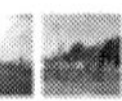
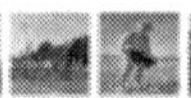

5.0km 20:30 4:05/km
Distance Moving Time Pace

Elevation 0m Calories 500
Elapsed Time 20:30

Device: Garmin Forerunner 220 Shoes: Brooks No idea My flamingo pink shoes (67.0 km)

9:04 AM on Saturday, August 29, 2015

Another terrible positive split, terrible running today, the immodium run

Changed too many things, pre race food, trainers (ultras almost too comfy for short fast race), no looking at my

...

| 5.0km | 20:25 | 4:04/km |
|---|---|---|
| Distance | Elapsed Time | Pace |

| | | | |
|---|---|---|---|
| Elevation | 0m | Calories | 500 |
| Moving Time | 20:25 | | |

Device: Garmin Forerunner 220 Shoes: Skechers Ultra (195.4 km)

9:04 AM on Saturday, September 5, 2015

Final slow taper, 1st time @Havant parkrun 23rd/262 with a negative split, some amazing fast kids here, 4 in top 10 !

Add a description

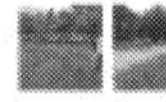
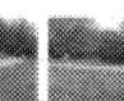

| 4.7km | 22:28 | 4:41/km |
|---|---|---|
| Distance | Moving Time | Pace |

| | | | |
|---|---|---|---|
| Elevation | 22m | Calories | 476 |
| Elapsed Time | 22:28 | | |

Device: Garmin Forerunner 220 Shoes: ASICS Fuji trail (9.7 km)

7:13 AM on Sunday, September 6, 2015

Duathlon part 1, focusing on even splits

Add a description

| 4.9km | 21:30 | 4:21/km |
|---|---|---|
| Distance | Elapsed Time | Pace |

| | | | |
|---|---|---|---|
| Elevation | 0m | Calories | 490 |
| Moving Time | 21:30 | | |

Device: Garmin Forerunner 220 Shoes: Skechers Go Run 4 (103.5 km)

7:37 AM on Sunday, September 6, 2015

Duathlon part 2, focusing on even splits

Add a description

2

STRAVA LABS
View Flybys ›

| 40.1km | 1:15:31 | 12m |
|---|---|---|
| Distance | Moving Time | Elevation |

| 177W | 802kJ |
|---|---|
| Estimated Avg Power | Energy Output |

| | Avg | Max |
|---|---|---|
| Speed | 31.9km/h | 38.5km/h |
| Cadence | 56 | 97 |
| Calories | 894 | |
| Elapsed Time | 1:16:05 | |

Show Less

Device: Garmin Forerunner 220 Bike: road bike

8:54 AM on Sunday, September 6, 2015

Duathlon part 3, focusing on even splits

Add a description

| 9.7km | 45:14 | 4:39/km |
|---|---|---|
| Distance | Elapsed Time | Pace |

| | | | |
|---|---|---|---|
| Elevation | 0m | Calories | 968 |
| Moving Time | 45:14 | | |

Device: Garmin Forerunner 220 Shoes: Skechers Go Run 4 (103.5 km)

9:10 AM on Saturday, September 12, 2015

**Parkrun Queen Elizabeth country park, 9th overall**

Dodgy knee today :(

| 4.9km | 22:22 | 4:29/km |
|---|---|---|
| Distance | Elapsed Time | Pace |

| | | | |
|---|---|---|---|
| Elevation | 113m | Calories | 504 |
| Moving Time | 22:22 | | |

Device: Garmin Forerunner 220 — Shoes: ASICS Fuji trail (9.7 km)

8:04 AM on Sunday, September 13, 2015

**Southern Sportive - longest ride by over 50k, got a gold medal finish time !**

Dickhead me uploaded the wrong course to my Garmin, left it late to hit gold time

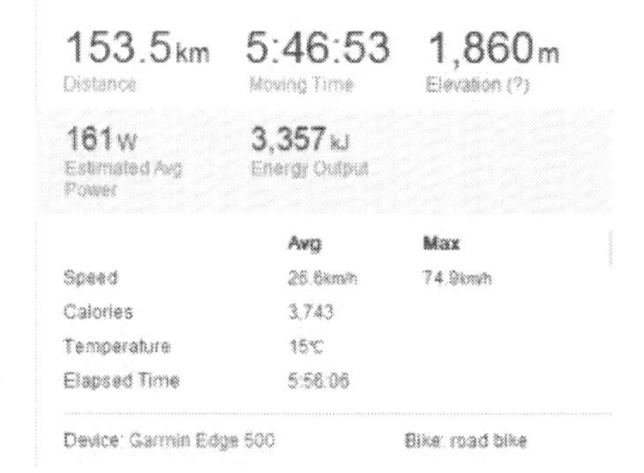

| 153.5km | 5:46:53 | 1,860m |
|---|---|---|
| Distance | Moving Time | Elevation (?) |

| 161w | 3,357kJ |
|---|---|
| Estimated Avg Power | Energy Output |

| | Avg | Max |
|---|---|---|
| Speed | 26.6km/h | 74.9km/h |
| Calories | 3,743 | |
| Temperature | 15℃ | |
| Elapsed Time | 5:56:06 | |

Device: Garmin Edge 500 — Bike: road bike

9:07 AM on Saturday, September 19, 2015

**QE parkrun, more new trainers,12th overall, 1st in age group plus a pb**

Add a description

| 5.0km | 22:13 | 4:26/km |
|---|---|---|
| Distance | Elapsed Time | Pace |

| | | | |
|---|---|---|---|
| Elevation | 113m | Calories | 505 |
| Moving Time | 22:13 | | |

Device: Garmin Forerunner 220 — Shoes: Salomon (27.4 km)

9:08 AM on Saturday, September 26, 2015

**Havant Parkrun pacing practice in my new trainers, another negative split on Garmin (Strava shows different? )**

| 4.9km | 21:51 | 4:25/km |
|---|---|---|
| Distance | Elapsed Time | Pace |

| | | | |
|---|---|---|---|
| Elevation | 31m | Calories | 491 |
| Moving Time | 21:51 | | |

Device: Garmin Forerunner 220 — Shoes: ASICS gel fuji runnegade (33.9 km)

12:29 PM on Sunday, September 27, 2015

**Butser Challenge fell race, downs were great incl segment record, ups were poor, achieved race time goal & met some friends, overall a good day**

Shoe laces came undone twice during km 6, Raynaud's syndrome makes this quite a difficult task - need elastic

| 7.9km | 46:30 | 5:50/km |
|---|---|---|
| Distance | Elapsed Time | Pace |

| | | | |
|---|---|---|---|
| Elevation | 350m | Calories | 871 |
| Moving Time | 46:30 | | |

Device: Garmin Forerunner 220 — Shoes: ASICS gel fuji runnegade (33.9 km)

9:04 AM on Saturday, October 3, 2015

Unplanned Havant parkrun, dodgy knee, terrible pacing, but new pb plus butternut squash pie as a reward

Add a description

| 4.8km | 21:36 | 4:25/km |
|---|---|---|
| Distance | Elapsed Time | Pace |

| | | | |
|---|---|---|---|
| Elevation | 25m | Calories | 485 |
| Moving Time | 21:36 | | |

Device: Garmin Forerunner 220 Shoes: ASICS gel fuji runnegade (33.9 km)

9:06 AM on Saturday, October 10, 2015

Havant Parkrun: Really painful cramps in both calves on a parkrun, what's going on ? Apple meringue pie this weekend

| 4.8km | 21:47 | 4:29/km |
|---|---|---|
| Distance | Elapsed Time | Pace |

| | | | |
|---|---|---|---|
| Elevation | 30m | Calories | 481 |
| Moving Time | 21:47 | | |

Device: Garmin Forerunner 220 Shoes: Salomon (27.4 km)

9:00 AM on Sunday, October 11, 2015

Chichester half 90/734, beat my goal time despite dodgy calf's, tried heart rate zone 4 racing for a change, felt weird not looking at pace, fell over yet again

| 21.1km | 1:42:39 | 4:51/km |
|---|---|---|
| Distance | Elapsed Time | Pace |

| | | | |
|---|---|---|---|
| Elevation | 213m | Calories | 2,107 |
| Moving Time | 1:42:39 | | |

Device: Garmin Forerunner 220 Shoes: Skechers Go Run 4 (103.5 km)

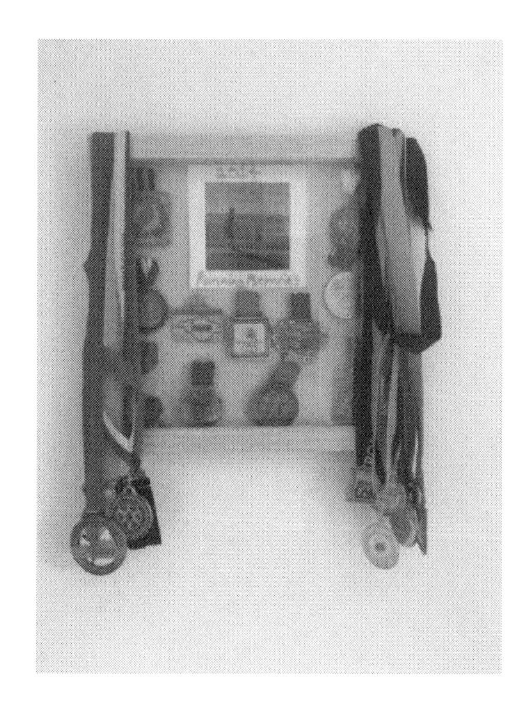

## Bonus section: What happened in year 3 – A short blog

So I ended my second book with this paragraph

To sum up, this year has been about going further than before with others, next year I'm going to try balancing this off with also going faster but alone. I don't know how I will manage this, I'm usually an all or nothing kind of person, but I'm hoping with my friends, work colleagues, and my own self-awareness, I will notice if I way too much back to the dark side. If I go into a silent mode for a short period then it's because I like my own thinking time, but if I turn into a self-obsessed idiot again feel free to tell me.

But also decided not to write a third instalment of my book, I did this because I know I am not a writer, I wrote a blog / diary which turned into an average book. My stories and achievements on the running side were good but not outstanding. I didn't want to write yet again about struggling with injuries, running races, and eating cake; it would have been boring which would be a shame since the book was meant to be inspiring.

So I've decided to go back to where this all started and write a short(ish) blog explaining what happened in 2016 and how I did with regards to the last paragraph in my book.

2016 started off well, no injuries and still fairly trim despite my Xmas excessive eating and drinking. I did my usual; no alcohol for the first few months, very little food treats, and just concentrated on fitness and work. I decided to ease into training by following a 5k plan to just get my legs moving faster. I entered several Parkruns & Great Run Local events, plus something called the Chilli Hilly cross country race. I hated the Chilli Hilly; it was just relentless mud on a wet and grim day. I've got better at accepting these conditions but I like to run with a smile on my face, I couldn't manage that in those conditions and was forever trying to maintain footing. I ended that race (10k'ish) 24th out of 239 runners which was okay, but I really should have pushed harder and finished higher up than that. The Parkruns were a totally different matter, the 5k training paid off, I hit PB's (sub 20 minutes) on 2 consecutive weekends at Southsea, and then in February went even faster (around 19m30s). I'd say that was one of my goals for the year completed, running fast but also alone.

I wanted an easy option for racing in 2016 so bought a season ticket for the Maverick trail series of races, that's 10 races throughout the year, all in the countryside, and all in different counties in the UK. The only thing I regret with these races was there was just one category for race results so oldies like me racing again kids was going to be a challenge when I wanted to achieve podiums. I also chucked in the Scott Snowdonia marathon as my big run for the year, the thought of running up and down Snowdon attracted me to this.

February was another month where I had a pb goal at the Worthing half marathon. I felt great leading up to this, problem was I felt great only based on a 5k training plan. The race went okay, I set a new 10 mile pb along the way @ 1 hr 8 min, but then the wheels fell off and I slowed down towards the end. I did end with a pb of around 1hr 32m, but the lack of longer training sessions really showed as I felt I should have gone under 1 hr 30m.

Happy with my pb successes I moved away from distance pb's and wanted to finish higher in races. I shifted to a longer half marathon training plan in preparation for the Maverick races (they have 3 distances at each race, usually around 5 mile, 10 mile and 13 mile). March was the first Maverick race in the New Forest, not really my favourite race as it was very flat, but on the plus side it was all cross country and possibly one of the wettest races I've done - we even had to run literally straight across rivers through the water. I remember at the Peak District Skyrace where I'd tip-toe through a puddle, but now I'm more than happy to just run straight through and enjoy the refreshment of the water on my legs. I completed the long distance in the Maverick race and finished in 14th place which I was happy with, I took a hard fall going downhill which knocked my confidence a bit but overall it was good.

April started with a Duathlon at the Goodwood car racing circuit, consisting of a 5k run, 40k bike, 10k run. This started off terribly, I had racked my bike and stood at the start line when all of a sudden a loud bang went off and it wasn't the start gun, it was the tyres on you know whose bike. I had super inflated by tyres, alas by too much, and the thing exploded. Thank god it didn't happen while I was racing; luckily there were bike mechanics on hand who changed the inner tube while I did the first run. The 5k training really helped here, I was around top 30 in the running, however my trusty steel framed 14 gear road bike really showed her frailties on the bike leg with me peddling as fast as I could yet being constantly overtaken and finishing the bike leg around 70th. I ended the race 25th place which was fine; I knew I had a great excuse to buy a new bike now.

April and May also had several Maverick races, I continued to get used to fuelling and pacing in these and always finished around 10th place, usually with a field of about 70-100 runners. The races were gradually getting hillier which suited me, I'm not a great uphill runner but I am a determined hiker, the downhill's were now my weakness following previous injuries, I just constantly have problems with my glutes and hamstrings and had picked up a new hip injury which meant I was hobbling a bit again. Cause for this injury wasn't running apparently, it was my day job getting in the way, I was stationed in the London office for 4 months and locked up in a hotel on work nights, the constant desk sitting and unfamiliar beds, combined with a total lack of any gym strengthening work, had caused my hips and legs to get lazy / weak, so the physio was back on the case fixing me. My training took a huge back seat at this point, I couldn't even cross train by cycling because I was away from home, so I would generally just turn up for races or cycle at weekends and that was it. I also completed my only Ultra Marathon of the year in April, it was a 6 hour run as far as you can event over a 5k out and back course, I actually only ran for 4hr 30m but it was enough to complete 51k and grab second place. This was a great race to take part in because it was the first event put on by 3 friends of mine, Claire, Kiernan and Del. I'm totally in awe of their achievements here, setting up a company (On The Whistle), arranging events, and making sure they are achievable for as many people as possible (for some just one out and back was a the longest they'd done), is inspiring.

It was while I was away that I also fell into a period of depression, caused firstly by being unhappy with work (I felt like I was lost with no real purpose at the time) plus time away from home didn't help. I took up the option of telephone counselling to help with this, it was the best thing I did because it made me take things out of my head and discuss them clearer with someone. Over time things did get better, mostly thanks to a combination of the time left in London reducing and the problems in my head were becoming less of a problem and more of an opportunity. People's attitude towards counselling surprise me, many thought it was weak to go ask for help, what they failed to see was they were incredibly weak on the inside while managing to maintain a brave face on the outside, whereas I felt I grew into someone far stronger as a result of this.

During June I also achieved another of my goals, a podium finish of 2nd place at the Maverick middle distance race in the Cotswolds. It was here I met a well-known runner called Duane Roberts and his wife, the plan was to do the long course with him but as soon as we had set off it was obvious I would damage myself going that far over a hilly course so I opted for middle distance and it turned out to be the correct decision.

July was the Snowden race, I was really worried about this as my leg was still knackered and I whilst I knew determination would get me through the 26.2 miles, I also knew the long term effects may have been more damage to my body. I thought back on why I entered this race, it was to run up and down a mountain, it wasn't about running 26 miles, so I did the wise thing and opted to drop down distances. Glad to say I did the right thing, the race was fantastic, it wasn't pretty, especially going downhill on the slate where I struggled and at one point had to opt to chuck myself to the ground and take a really heavy fall rather than literally running over the edge of the mountain. I finished in one piece 79th out of 360, and Sally and I enjoyed a long weekend in Llanberis exploring a beautiful corner of Wales. This was our first trip to Wales, I loved it.

August and September were yet more Maverick races including an epic in Somerset where we used AirBnB to stay overnight and then moved onto the Brecon Beacons for a few more days of exploring. What an amazing place that was, really friendly, great mountains and scenery, loads of hiking completed with Sally. I also completed my first night race, a half marathon called Roam Day into Night. I got 2nd place in this race, as well as a 3rd place at a Maverick race, still no podium but at least I was improving.

October I went for another goal, I'd always said I didn't want to enter the same race twice as I didn't care about pb's however this year was different so I entered the Chichester half marathon again. Experience of knowing the course really showed here, I knocked 6 minutes off last years' time and finished 44th out of 747 runners.

I then went for another first and competed in the Great South Run, a flat 10 mile race on concrete around Southsea/Portsmouth, not the most inspiring race in my head but I just had to do it so I could say I tried. I ran with an old school friend of mine whose goal was to finish in 70 minutes, I knew I could manage this because I'd done 10 miles in 68 minutes at the Worthing half, this was before all my injuries but psychologically I knew it was possible. I finished the race in 69 minutes, despite the great crowds I was a little bored by the scenery and didn't find the motivation to kick on at the end; my splits were even all the way through. Unfortunately I finished without Nick who tailed off a little towards the end but still ended with a respectable time of 72 minutes.

October is my birthday so I at last treated myself to a new carbon fibre bike, it's not a mega expensive bike but it is probably worth more than my 11 year old car. What a difference it makes with 22 gears and 4kg weight loss vs my old bike, I love my bike. I struggled to adapt to so many gears so bought a cadence senor and found it much easier to select gears using this, I focus on cadence around 80 to 90 and as soon as I go outside this range I change gears.

Rest of the year has been a first for me, no races since the Great South Run; I've focussed on strength work in the gym and cross training on my bike, plus a bit of swimming. I've not lost weight yet but I'm feeling really good. I'm currently weighing around 83kg, have a small issue with my right leg/glute (apparently it's sciatica but it's been hanging around for ages now), so I've promised myself that at least one of these two things need to improve before I reward myself with a hard race again. I have also changed jobs, still with the same company but now doing projects within Group HR. This year with my exploring the countryside has meant my whole outlook of work/life has changed, I enjoy my job and like working for the company, but I think I need to find something which enables me to focus more on what I enjoy outside of work more. The counselling helped with this, ironically the counselling was provided by work and yet made me question my future career/job plans. Don't get me wrong, I still enjoy my job, the company is changing but it's still a great place to work, and I will still do my best at it, but I would say I have changed as a person and now love my life outside of work even more know and that's tipping the balance a bit, especially as I get older and realise life is too short to keep putting off future plans. I find myself addicted to watching programmes like Countryfile and The Adventure Show, I've been inspired by some of my AirBnB hosts, and I have strange dreams about owning a smaller house but also having rooms for guests to stay, Sally feeding them cake and me taking them out to explore the local areas - I think this is all leading me somewhere in the future.

I also published my book in paperback which was a nice thing to achieve, I've even signed copies for people and donated copies to charities, which makes me feel good inside.

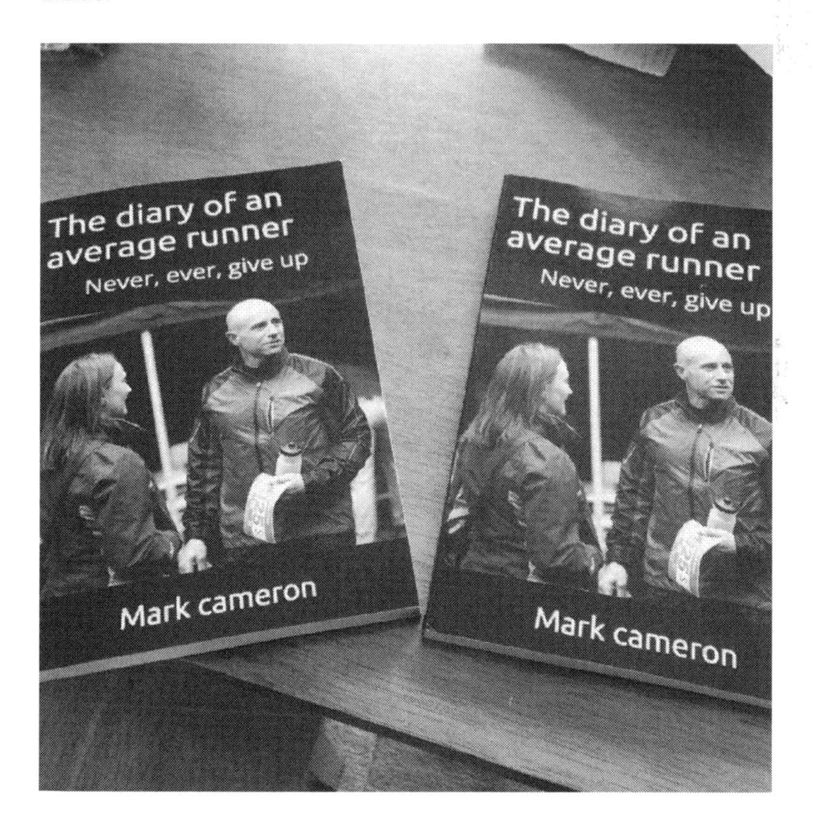


Focus for next year, continue training smarter, run less and stop pushing my body so hard, it's falling to pieces too easy as I get older, and instead focus on diet and get under 80kg (ideally 75-80 kg range). I think this will make a huge impact on my training as well as health, I'm secretly hoping to convert my 2nd and 3rd places into a 1st place at some point. I also want to continue exploring the UK, either on foot running or hiking, or cycling on my new bike. Whilst the pb's and podiums were great this year, I've also really loved weekends away with Sally visiting new places. I don't need a race to do this, I can just do a bit of research of explore without running with others. I'd love to cycle further than I've done before, Brecon to Snowden sounds ideal, maybe I will find some fool to come along with me. I'm going to race abroad, almost certainly the Madeira Skyrace (21k option), and also enter another series of trail races (just 3 in this series, Dartmoor, Exmoor and Brecon, options of 10k up to 50k in each), and finally a couple of Maverick races.

That's it, probably the longest blog in the world, a whole years' worth while I couldn't be bothered to put into a book but looking at the length of this probably would have been easy to copy and paste into a book. It's been a great year, success on my feet, success at work, fabulous time away with Sally, met a load of new inspiring people, and enjoyed loads of amazing home baked cakes to keep me fuelled up; I really hope the year has been just as good for yourselves.

**The end**

**Please now rate this book on Amazon!!**

**#Thankyou**

Printed in Poland
by Amazon Fulfillment
Poland Sp. z o.o., Wrocław